Creative Decorating with Ribbons

Creative Decorating
with Ribbons

Mary Jo Hiney
Marinda Stewart
Katheryn Tidwell Foutz
Vanessa-Ann

Sterling Publishing Co., New York
A Sterling/Chapelle Book

Chapelle, Ltd.

Owner: Jo Packham
Editor: Laura Best

Staff: Marie Barber, Areta Bingham, Malissa Boatwright, Kass Burchett, Rebecca Christensen, Holly Fuller, Marilyn Goff, Michael Hannah, Shirley Heslop, Holly Hollingsworth, Susan Jorgensen, Leslie Liechty, Pauline Locke, Ginger Mikkelsen, Barbara Milburn, Linda Orton, Karmen Quinney, Rhonda Rainey, Leslie Ridenour, and Cindy Stoeckl

Photographer: Kevin Dilley for Hazen Photography
Photography Styling: Susan Laws

A special thank you to C.M. Offray & Son, Inc., who provided all ribbons used in this book.

Library of Congress Cataloging-in-Progress Data Available

10 9 8 7 6 5 4 3 2 1

Published by Sterling Publishing Company, Inc.
387 Park Avenue South, New York, NY 10016
©1998 by Chapelle Ltd.
Distributed in Canada by Sterling Publishing
c/o Canadian Manda Group, One Atlantic Avenue, Suite 105
Toronto, Ontario, Canada M6K 3E7
Distributed in Great Britain and Europe by Cassell PLC
Wellington House, 125 Strand
London WCR2 0BB, England
Distributed in Australia by Capricorn Link (Australia) Pty Ltd.
P.O. Box 6651, Baulkham Hills, Business Centre
NSW 2153, Australia

Printed in Hong Kong
All Rights Reserved

Sterling ISBN 0-8069-9708-7

If you have any questions or comments please contact:
Chapelle, Ltd., Inc.
P.O. Box 9252
Ogden, UT 84409
(801) 621-2777
(801) 621-2788 Fax

Ribbon Work

Ribbon work is a centuries-old needle art that has been used to adorn women's garments throughout history. Although there are few historic documents on the subject of ribbon work, this fascinating needle art has been rediscovered. Today ribbon crafting is a means of expressing creativity.

The adorned pillows, frames, and elegant keepsakes featured in this book are excellent examples of the beauty that can be achieved when creating by inspiration and mixing together several different techniques and mediums.

By using basic embroidery stitches and dimensional ribbon work techniques, combined with taffeta wire-edge ribbon, satin ribbon, metallic ribbons, antique laces, and more, the author fashions delicate floral sprays that offer a pleasant blend of textures and colors.

The ribbon flowers in this book do not require the use of any unusual tools or equipment. The ribbon color, size, and texture, combined with construction techniques for different petals, determine the shape and appearance of each flower created. The wire-edge ribbon helps keep the flowers resilient. Wire-edge ribbon flowers can be shaped and reshaped as desired.

The key to ribbon work is maintaining control over the ribbon. Understanding what each ribbon length will do is of utmost importance in creating petals and flowers.

Create a dimensional masterpiece by combining the fine artistry of ribbon work with the amazing technique of transferring actual pieces of art to fabric and other project surfaces.

Let creativity bloom by substituting different ribbons for those suggested and combining flowers to design original arrangements.

Table of

Contents

Embroidery Work Basics

Ribbon Tips

Always keep ribbon flat and loose while working stitches. Untwist ribbon often and pull ribbon softly so it lies flat on top of fabric. Be creative with stitching. Exact stitch placement is not critical, but make certain any placement marks are covered.

Needles

A size 3 crewel embroidery needle works well for most fabrics when using 4mm ribbon. For 7mm ribbon, use a chenille needle, size 18 to 24. As a rule of thumb, the barrel of the needle must create a hole in the fabric large enough for ribbon to pass through. If ribbon does not pull through fabric easily, a larger needle is needed.

Floss

Floss colors are outlined in project stitch guides. Separate floss into one or more strands according to project instructions.

Threading Ribbon on Needle

Thread ribbon through eye of needle. With tip of needle, pierce center of ribbon ¼" from end. Pull remaining ribbon through to lock ribbon on needle.

Knotting End of Ribbon

1. Drape ribbon in a circular manner to position end of ribbon perpendicular to tip of needle. Pierce end of ribbon with needle. Pierce again ¼" up ribbon.
2. Pull needle and ribbon through to form a knot at end of ribbon.

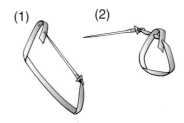

(1)   (2)

Ending Stitching

Secure stitches in place for each small area. Do not drag ribbon from one area to another. Tie a slip knot on the wrong side of needle work to secure stitch in place and end ribbon.

Note: Please refer to a book on basic embroidery stitches to complete projects in this book that may require embroidery work.

Tool Basics

Fabric Scissors

Designate a pair of scissors for cutting fabrics and non-wire edge ribbons. Using fabric scissors to cut other materials will dull blades and make them less effective at cutting fabric.

Hot Glue Gun & Glue Sticks

Hot glue is best for constructing projects. Use the "cloudy" glue sticks when working with fabric. Clear glue sticks do not penetrate fabric very well.

Marking Tools

Marking tools include an air- or water-soluble dressmaker's pen, and an erasable marking pen. Use marking tools to mark general placement. Try to use as few marks as possible-too many marks can be confusing.

Transferring

Materials
Tracing paper
Transfer paper

Tools
Marking tools:
    disappearing pen;
    dressmaker's pen;
    erasable pen; pencil
Photocopy machine
Scissors: craft; fabric
Straight pins
Tape of choice

1.   If directions indicate to enlarge pattern, place pattern directly in photo-copy machine. Enlarge required percentage.
2.   If using natural light-box technique, trace design on a piece of tracing paper or mylar. Tape tracing paper onto a sun-lit window. Hold or tape fabric in place over design and trace design onto fabric with marking tool of choice.
3.   Color photocopies can be transferred to project in three steps. Brush photo transfer medium on color photocopy. Press medium side down on project as desired and allow to dry. Remove paper using a wet sponge or following manufacturer's instructions.

Transferring Basics

Artwork provided in this book is to be used for transferring directly to paper, fabric, and other surfaces. Copy artwork from this book and enlarge as indicated at a professional copy center.

Photo Transfer Medium
Transfer color photocopies to any project in three steps. Brush medium on color photocopy. Press medium side down on project as desired and allow to dry. Remove paper using a wet sponge or as directed in manufacturer's instructions.

Transferring Art to Fabric

Heat Transferring
Copy artwork using photo transfer paper purchased at a crafts store, and a color laser copier at a professional copy center. Trim to ¼" around transfer. Set iron to highest and driest setting. Preheat fabric where transfer will be positioned until area is hot. Place transfer in position with image side down while fabric is still hot. Iron lightly over transfer for 20 seconds. Iron, applying heavy even pressure to transfer for three minutes. Peel off paper backing while still hot.

Dimensional Ribbon Work

Stem Work
It is recommended that a small loop be bent in one end of wire before inserting it into the flower. Secure wire with a dab of craft glue.

Baste Stitch
Make a baste stitch with thread using long, even running stitches. The lines of basting serve as a guide for positioning main elements and shapes or for adhering two fabrics together temporarily.

Basic Bud
Make a point by crossing one end of a length of ribbon down and across other end of ribbon.

Apple Blossom
1.   Evenly space five pulled petals specified in project's instructions around stamen attached to stem. Wrap base of petals securely with wire to hold. Attach to stem wire as project instructions specify to simulate a branch.
2.   Completed Apple Blossom.

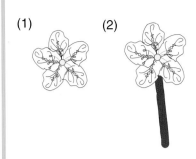

(1) (2)

Bachelor Button

1.   Stitch raw edges together allowing ⅛" seam allowance. Gather ribbon.
2.   Gather one edge of ribbon tightly. Knot to secure.
3.   Insert stem wire with stamens attached through center. Wrap stem wire with green florist tape.
4.   Completed Bachelor Button.

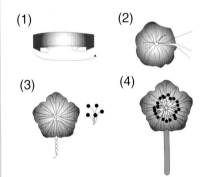

(1) (2)

(3) (4)

Bead Stringing

Knot thread and/or bring needle and thread to front of fabric. Thread on desired number of beads. Reverse needle and string back through pervious beads to the first. Knot thread again or take needle back through original hole on fabric and tie off on back.

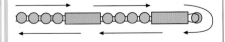

Bleeding Heart

1.   Stitch raw edges, using a ⅛" seam allowance, to create a tube. Turn raw edges to the inside.
2.   Gather-stitch around top edge of ribbon and pull tightly. Knot to secure.
3.   Gather-stitch around lower edge ¼" from edge of ribbon. Insert a small amount of fiberfill or cotton ball. Pull gathers tightly to create a ruffle. Knot off to secure.
4.   Glue stamens into ruffled end for completed Bleeding Heart.

(1)

(2)

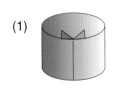

(3)

(4)

Boat Leaf

1.   Fold ribbon in half lengthwise.
2.   Fold both ends of ribbon at 45 degree angle.

3.   Gather-stitch down one angle, across the bottom and up the other angle. Pull threads loosely. Knot to secure. Trim excess ribbon from folded angles. Open ribbon.
4.   Completed Boat Leaf.

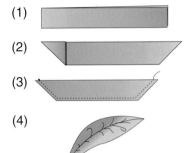

(1)

(2)

(3)

(4)

Buckram Rose

1.   Slash buckram circle to center.
2.   Overlap and stitch to hold.
3.   Turn under one end of ribbon ¼" and stitch on three sides over center of buckram cone with double thread.
4.   Fold ribbon on bias across cone to top right corner. Stitch across width of ribbon to secure.
5.   Continue folding on bias and stitching across width in thirds or quarters across cone.
6.   Never cover center or previous folds completely.
7.   When cone is covered, trim remaining ribbon and stitch to back of buckram. Add leaves if desired.
8.   Completed Buckram Cone.

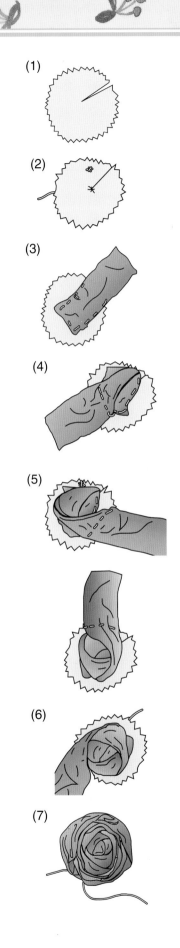

(1)

(2)

(3)

(4)

(5)

(6)

(7)

(8)

Calyx

1. Fold ribbon ⅛" under on one raw edge.
2. Secure unfolded edge to stem of previously constructed flower with a dab of glue.
3. Place a small line of glue along top edge of ribbon. Glue in a circle around underside of flower. Overlap folded edge to cover raw edges. Twist bottom open end of ribbon around stem wire. Cover with florist tape to finish.
4. Completed Calyx.

(1)

(2)   (3)   (4)

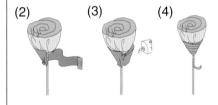

Cascading

Tie a bow near center in length of ribbon. Attach bow to project using hot glue or needle and coordinating thread, making small tacking stitches. Loosely loop and twist ribbon tails around design as indicated in project instructions, randomly tacking to project as desired.

Circular Ruffle

1. Fold ribbon in half, matching cut ends. Seam cut ends.
2. Gather-stitch along selvage. Pull gathers tightly and secure thread.
3. Completed Circular Ruffle.

(1)

(2)

(3)

Doily Flower

1. Fold doily in half, then in thirds.
2. Fold bottom corner over. Glue bottom folded rolled edge to hold it in place. Place thin bead of glue around center of second doily. Fold up around glue to slightly ruffle second doily. Glue first doily into center of second doily.
3. Completed Doily Flower.

(1)

(2)   (3)

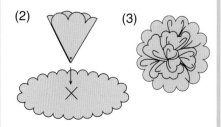

Fluting

Attach one ribbon end to fabric. Fold down diagonally and glue. Fold up and down diagonally again and glue. Repeat for entire area to be fluted. Fluting should extend ¼" past edge to be fluted.

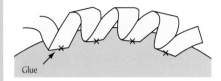

Glue

Fold-Over Leaf

1. Fold right half of ribbon length forward diagonally.
2. At center of fold, fold back left half of ribbon. Gather-stitch across bottom edge of ribbon ends.
3. Tightly pull gather stitch and secure thread for a completed Fold-Over Leaf.

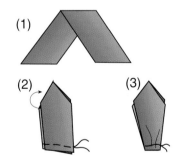

(1)

(2) (3)

Folded Flower

1. Beginning with ribbon end facing downward, fold ribbon diagonally and forward and back so fold is about 1" deep. Fold again diagonally forward and back, as for first fold. Pin bottom folded edge for better control. After ten folds have been pinned, gather-stitch along bottom edge. Remove

pins after stitching. Fold, pin, and stitch another ten petals until entire length of ribbon has been stitched. Tightly gather and secure thread. Straighten folds so all are facing same direction.
2. Beginning at one end, roll folds into flower. Secure on underside as needed to keep rolls in place. Completed Folded Flower.

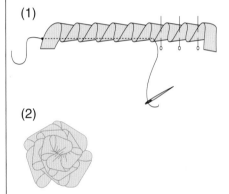

(1)

(2)

Folded Leaf

1. Fold ends of one ribbon length forward diagonally.
2. Gather-stitch across bottom edge of folds.
3. Tightly pull gather stitch and secure thread for a completed Folded Leaf.

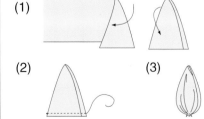

(1)

(2)   (3)

Folded & Rolled Rose

1. Cut a length of ribbon. Fold one end of the ribbon down at a right angle, creating a post to hold onto.
2. Fold the folded end in half. Stitch this in place

securely with thread. Roll and fold ribbon.
3. Continue rolling and folding ribbon as shown, stitching to secure.
4. Upon folding and rolling at least half of the length of ribbon, hand-stitch a gathering stitch along bottom edge of remaining length of ribbon. Pull gathers tightly and wrap gathered section around folded rose. Stitch in place to secure.

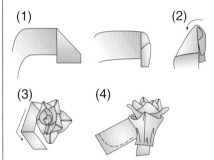

(1)   (2)

(3)   (4)

Fork Cut

1. Fold desired ribbon in half lengthwise.
2. Cut end of ribbon diagonally from corner point on selvage edge.
3. Completed Fork Cut.

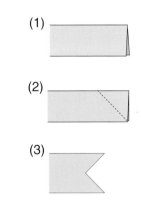

(1)

(2)

(3)

Forsythia

1. Fold two ribbons in half. Insert a 3" piece of paddle wire in fold of ribbons.

2. Twist wire tightly around ribbons to secure. Cover twisted wire with brown tape. Repeat Steps 1 and 2 for specified number of forsythia flowers.

3. Completed Forsythia.

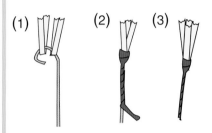

(1)　(2)　(3)

Gathered Leaf

1. Fold ribbon in half, matching short ends. Gather-stitch along edge.

2. Pull to gather and secure thread. Open and shape leaf.

3. Completed Gathered Leaf.

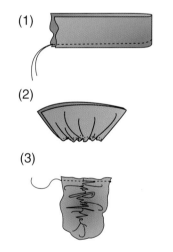

(1)

(2)

(3)

Gathered Rose

1. Fold one short edge of ribbon at a right angle.

2. Fold point back to ribbon keeping bottoms even.

3. Roll folded end of ribbon and secure with thread. Gather-stitch half of remaining ribbon. Pull thread and wrap gather

---

around folded ribbon.

4. Gather-stitch remaining ribbon. Wrap gather around.

5. Completed Gathered Rose.

(1)
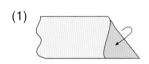

(2)
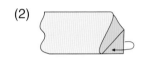

(3)

(4)
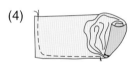

(5)

Gathered Ruffle Flower

1. Gather-stitch along selvage edge. Pull gathers as tightly as possible and secure thread.

2. Slightly overlap and tack ribbon ends together for a completed Gathered Ruffle Flower.

(1)

(2)

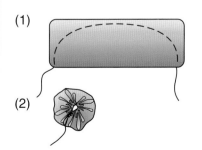

Knotted Mum

1. Cut ribbon to desired length. Tie knot at center of each length. Fold in half and pin ends.

2. Place knotted petals side by side and sew together with gathering stitch, taking desired seam. Pull gathers as tightly as possible and secure thread.

3. Completed Knotted Mum.

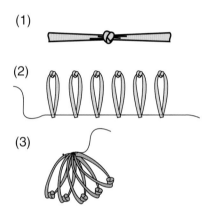

(1)

(2)

(3)

Large Flower

1. Mark ribbon as instructions state.

2. Fold ribbon diagonally at marks, securing with pins. Stitch a gathering stitch along outside edge. Pull tightly to gather.

3. Completed Large Flower.

(1)

(2)

(3)

Lily

1.   Surround one brown chenille stamen with six yellow chenille stamens. Using paddle wire, attach to top of 12" piece of stem wire.
2.   Attach three petals, evenly spaced around stamens, with seam side upward. Attach three more petals, evenly spaced between first three petals. Wrap base of petals tightly with wire to hold. Cover with dk. green stem tape. Attach two leaves to stem of flower wrapping with green florist tape.
3.   Completed Lily.

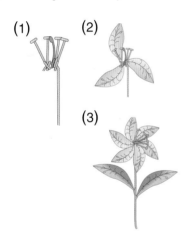

Mountain Fold

Fold desired length of ribbon diagonally back and forth, forming desired number of mountain-shaped folds. Pin bottom fold edge for better control. Gather-stitch along bottom edge, removing pins after stitching. Pull gathers as tightly as possible and secure thread.

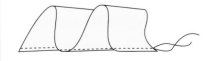

Multi-Loop Bow

1.   Leaving a length of ribbon for one tail, make a figure eight with desired size loops. Hold ribbon in center with thumb and forefinger and make second figure eight on top of first.
2.   Continue until desired number of loops are formed and leave a second tail. Pinch together center of loops.
3.   Wrap and knot craft wire around center to secure for completed Multi-Loop Bow.

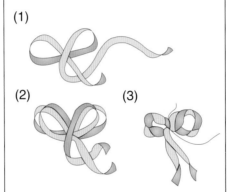

Multiple Petal Section

1.   Using a disappearing-ink fabric marker, mark a length of ribbon at four equal intervals, beginning and ending ¼" from raw ends. Run a hand-gathering stitch in a semicircular shape within each interval.
2.   Pull the gathering thread tightly so that each petal measures about the same. Knot thread to secure.

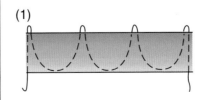

Narcissus

1.   Make Stitched Flower on page 17. Insert stem wire into stitched flower.
2.   Cut ⅞" orange ombré wire edge ribbon into five 4" lengths. Refer to Trumpet on page 17 for making center of flower. Stop after step 2.
3.   Cut ⅞" green ombré wire-edged ribbon into five 4" lengths. Refer to Calyx on page 11 and attach to underside of each flower.
4.   Make quantity of leaves specified in project instructions, referring to Boat Leaf on page 10. Attach leaf to stem by wrapping with green florist tape.
5.   Completed Narcissus.

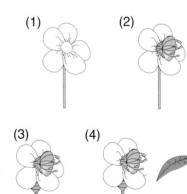

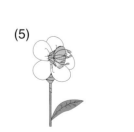

Pansy

1. Cut ribbon to desired length. Fold one long edge down. Pin to hold. Mark intervals.
2. Fold on marks. Gather-stitch. Pull thread as tightly as possible. Secure thread. Join petals together.
3. Completed Pansy.

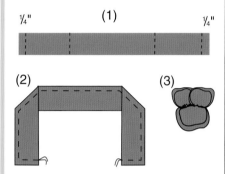

¼" (1) ¼"

(2) (3)

Pointed Petal or Leaf

1. Cut ribbon to desired length. Overlap ends of ribbon.
2. Gather-stitch at bottom edge.
3. Gather tightly to form petal. Wrap thread around stitches to secure. Trim excess ⅛" past stitching.
4. Do not trim if making a chain of Pointed Petals or Leaves. Completed Pointed Petal or Leaf.

(1)

(2)

(3)

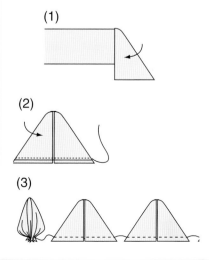

(4)

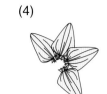

Variations:

A. No-Sew: Cut ribbon a little longer than needed. Fold ribbon as shown in Diagram 1. Twist ends as shown in Diagram A. Attach twist of petal/leaf to stem wire as shown in Diagram B.

(A)

B. Cluster: Cluster 5-9 pointed petals/leaves the length of stem wire. Attach to stem wire with floral tape.

(B)

Pulled Petal or Leaf

1. Fold wired ribbon length in half. matching raw edges.
2. Push ½" to ¾" of ribbon back on wires on one side. Pull wires evenly until gathered. Overlap ends of wires. Twist to secure.
3. Open and shape leaf for a completed Pulled Petal or Leaf.

(1)

(2) (3)

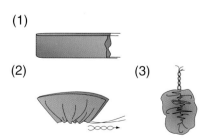

Ribbon Weaving

1. Transfer the pattern onto a sheet of paper and lay it right side up on work surface (a sheet of foam core or cardboard is recommended). Lay fusible webbing over pattern. Arrange ribbons side by side in a lengthwise direction in neat straight lines; pin or tape in place along the top edge. Also pin or tape the bottom edge about 1" below the pattern outline. Continue to lay strips of ribbon until the entire pattern has been covered. Repeat this process in a crosswise direction, pinning the left side edge only and leaving the right side free for weaving.
2. Weave ribbons one at a time over and under each lengthwise strip. To ease weaving, thread each ribbon length on a large blunt needle. Another trick is to take a bamboo skewer and weave it over and under the ribbons, creating a space to easily thread the ribbon through. After weaving is finished, fuse ribbons together with iron-on fusible webbing, following manufacturer's instructions. Remove pins and tape as the edges are pressed. Remove the woven ribbons from the work surface and cut pattern along edge and stitch as desired.

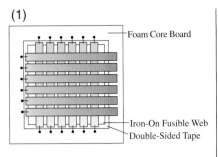

(1)

Foam Core Board

Iron-On Fusible Web
Double-Sided Tape

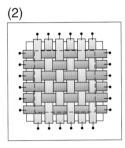

(2)

Rose

1. Knot one end of length of wired ribbon.

2. At opposite end, gently pull wire from one side to gather. Continue gathering ruffled and curling naturally. Leave wire end free; do not cut off.

3. To form rose, hold knotted end in one hand and begin to spiral gathered ribbon loosely around knot with other hand. Wrap tightly at first to form a bud, then continue wrapping lightly so that it flares out and acquires an open rose effect. To end, fold raw edge down to meet gathered edge. Secure by wrapping wire length around knot tightly and catching in free end; cut wire end off.

4. Completed Rose.

(1)

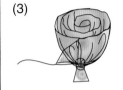

(2)

(3)

(4)

Variations:

A. Double Rose: Knot one end of ribbon. Pull both wires evenly to gather both sides of ribbon. Complete rose as instructed.

B. Antique Rose: Crush rose with palm of hand or wad in a ball in fist, then gently open, retaining as many folds as desired.

C. Crinkled Rose: After ribbon is gathered, but before wrapped into rose shape, finger pleat top edge of ribbon. Complete as instructed.

Rosette

1. Beginning at one end, fold end forward at right angle. Fold vertical end of ribbon forward upon itself.

2. Fold horizontal end of ribbon back and at right angle. Fold vertical ribbon over once. Continue folding ribbon forming the rosette.

3. Upon reaching center mark, secure with a stitch, leaving needle and thread attached. Gather-stitch

bottom edge of remaining ribbon. Gather tightly. Wrap gathered ribbon around bud.

4. Completed Rosette.

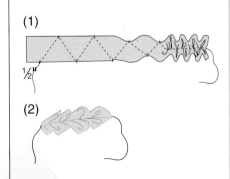

(1)

(2)

(3)

(4)

Ruching

1. Starting ½" from one end on one side of ribbon, mark 1" equal intervals. Starting 1" from same end on other side of ribbon, mark equal 1" intervals. Gather-stitch, connecting dots, from side to side, in a zigzag fashion.

2. Pull gathers and secure thread. Completed Ruched Ribbon.

(1)

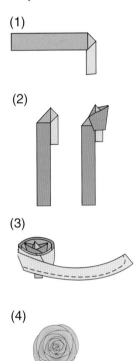

½"

(2)

Seed Pod

1. Stitch raw edges, using ⅛" seam allowance, to create a tube. Turn raw edges to the inside.
2. Gather-stitch around top edge of ribbon and pull tightly. Knot to secure.
3. Gather-stitch around lower edge ⅛" from edge of ribbon. Insert a small amount of fiberfill or cotton ball. Pull gathers tightly. Knot off to secure.
4. Completed Seed Pod.

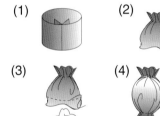

(1) (2) (3) (4)

Single Petal

1. Run a gathering stitch along sides and one long edge of a length of ribbon.
2. Pull the gathering thread tightly until the ribbon is ruffled. Knot thread to secure. Repeat to make as many petals as required.
Note: For a smooth, rounded petal, length of ribbon should equal width of ribbon multiplied by three. For a cupped petal, length should equal width multiplied by two. For a very ruffled petal, length should equal width multiplied by four.

(1)

(2)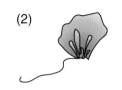

Spiral Rosetta

1. Gather-stitch along selvage edge and raw edges.
2. Pull gathers and secure thread. To form rose, hold one end in one hand and begin to spiral gathered ribbon loosely around end with other hand. Wrap tightly at first to form a bud, then continue wrapping lightly so that it flares out and acquires an open rose effect. Secure by stitching through gathered edge several times.
3. Completed Spiral Rosetta.

(1)

(2)   (3)

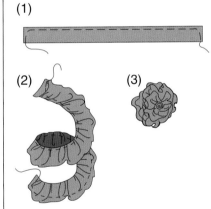

Squared-Off Petal

1. Run a gathering-stitch along three sides of ribbon. The length of the gathered ribbon needs to be greater than width of ribbon. Pull thread to gather and secure.

2. Completed Squared-Off Petal.

(1)

(2)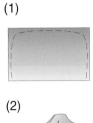

Stacked Bow

1. Fold ribbon back and forth as desired. Gather-stitch down center of stacked bow. Tightly gather and secure thread.
2. Completed Stacked Bow.

(1)

(2)

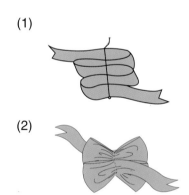

Stitched Flower

1. Fold ribbon according to project instructions. Gather-stitch down one side, across the bottom, up one side of fold and down the other side of fold. Repeat for specified number of petals. Gather into a circle. Stitch petals together to hold.
2. Completed Stitched Flower.

(1)

(2)

Tendril

1. Holding a length of wired ribbon at one end, begin twisting the ribbon in one direction until tight.
2. Ribbon will twist on itself for a completed Tendril.

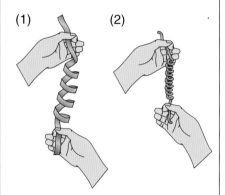

(1)   (2)

Trumpet

1. Stitch raw edges, using ⅛" seam allowance, to create a tube. Turn raw edges to the inside.
2. Gather-stitch around top edge of ribbon and pull tightly. Knot to secure.
3. Gather-stitch around lower edge ½" from edge of ribbon. Leave an opening 1" to 1¼" in diameter. Knot to secure. Turn back bottom edge and open into a ruffle.
4. Glue stamens into ruffled end for a completed Trumpet.

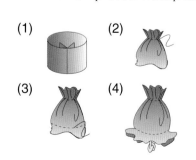

(1)   (2)

(3)   (4)

Twisted Rosebud

1. Hold ribbon between thumb and forefinger of left hand. Wrap ribbon around tip of forefinger to create a small cone.
2. Continue wrapping ribbon around fingertip giving ribbon a half twist inward every 1"-½". Wrap entire length of twisted ribbon around fingertip. Remove bud from finger. Fold loose ends into center of bud.
3. Completed Twisted Rosebud.

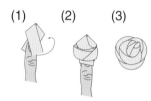

(1)   (2)   (3)

Wrapped Bud

1. Cut a length of ribbon. Lay a previously made Basic Bud in the center of the ribbon length.
2. Cross one end of ribbon down and across other end of ribbon, wrapping bud. Run a gathering stitch across this wrapped piece.
3. Pull the gathering thread tightly and wrap the thread around the base. Knot to secure. Completed Wrapped Bud.

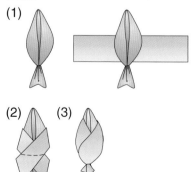

(1)

(2)   (3)

Painting Techniques

—Base

To base paint an area, apply two to three even coats of acrylic paint. This will ensure best coverage and an even look to paint.

—Dry-brush

Dip brush into paint. Work out paint on dry paper towel until almost no paint is visible when brushing. Brush on project in circles, starting in the center and working outward, releasing pressure while painting.

—Line

Outline a project, or areas within a project, using a liner brush. Line thickness is determined by amount of paint loaded on brush.

—Wash

Mix paint with water in a 1:3 ratio. Apply this paint wash to sealed wood. Several coats of light wash produce a soft, but deep, transparent color. Allow wash to dry between coats. If wash causes wood grain to raise, lightly sand washed surfaces before applying additional coats.

Mary Jo Hiney

Mary Jo Hiney's love of age-old needle arts evolved from sewing skills that she learned from her mother. Having mastered the basics, Mary Jo's creativity blossomed after attending the Fashion Institute of Design and Merchandising in Los Angeles. Following graduation, she worked in the downtown Los Angeles garment industry before beginning her stint in the wardrobe departments of many Hollywood studios. There she performed duties as a "dresser" for live television. Mary Jo's background in the garment industry and as a costumer has given her an unusual frame of reference that mixes reality with the dramatic.

Today, Mary Jo is the author of many "how to" books and articles as well as a designer for various companies in the craft industry. Teaching ribbon embroidery, ribbon work, and box-making around the world keeps her very busy. Mary Jo's primary motivation has always been to promote the beauty of creativity.

Pewter Frame

Note: Please refer to a book on basic embroidery stitches to complete this project.

Materials

Pewter frame: small with
  3" x 4" opening
Fabric: moiré, mauve, (¼ yd.)
Embroidery ribbon: 4mm
  lt. lavender (¾ yd.), dk.
  lavender (1¼ yds.), olive
  green (1¼ yds.), dk. olive
  green (½ yd.), dk. rose (¾ yd.)
Taffeta ribbon: 1½"-wide,

mauve (1 yd.)
Wire-edge ribbon: ⅝"-wide
green/peach/rose ombré
  (⅞ yd.); ⅞"-wide green
  ombré (⅝ yd.)
Ribbon roses: premade,
  small, cinnamon (2)
Cording: ⅛"-wide, mauve
  (¼ yd.)
Poster board: 4" x 5"
Quilt batting: 4" x 5"

General Supplies & Tools

Glue: craft
Needles: hand-sewing
Pen: disappearing ink
Pencil
Scissors: craft; fabric
Thread: coordinating

Instructions

1. Remove back and glass from pewter frame. Discard glass. Using pencil, trace an opening that is ⅛" larger than frame opening onto poster-board. Using craft scissors, cut out opening from poster board and set aside.

2. Refer to General Instructions for Transferring on page 9. Center and trace pewter frame opening onto wrong side of mauve moiré fabric.

3. Using hand-sewing needle and coordinating thread, baste-stitch on traced line. Refer to Pewter Frame Transfer Pattern on page 21. Center pattern and, using disappearing pen, transfer design to right side of fabric. Embroider design, following Pewter Frame Stitch Guide on page 21.

Pewter Frame Transfer Pattern

Pewter Frame Stitch Guide

Description	Ribbon	Stitch
1. Bud	dk. Lavender	Bullion Lazy Daisy
2. Bud	dk. Rose	1-Twist Ribbon Stitch
3. Leaf	olive Green	1-Twist Ribbon Stitch
4. Bud	lt. Lavender	French Knot (2 wraps)

4. Using craft glue, lightly glue quilt batting to poster board. Using fabric scissors, trim quilt batting flush with poster board's edge, slightly beveling quilt batting inward.

5. Trim embroidered moiré fabric ¾" larger than basting stitching. Center and snugly wrap embroidered moiré fabric around poster board. Trim all bulk and secure fabric edges to poster board with glue. Place poster board into frame opening and replace frame backing to close.

6. Cut green/peach/rose ombré wire-edge ribbon in two 7½" lengths. Using Pattern A circle, trace five half-circles onto each ribbon, leaving ¼" on each side of first and last traced half circles as shown in Diagram A. Gather-stitch along traced circles. Tightly gather to form petals; secure thread.

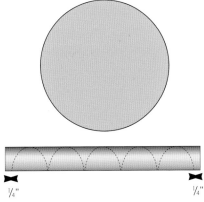

¼"   ¼"

Pattern A/Diagram A

7. Shape ribbon so five rose petals are on one edge and five green petals are on opposite edge. Join first petal to last at seam to form flower. Secure thread. Cup petals downward. Glue onto embroidery, referring to Pewter Frame Stitch Guide for placement.

8. Cut an 18" length of olive green and dk. olive green embroidery ribbon. Hold together, tie as one into 1½"-wide bow. Knot ribbon tails. Glue bow underneath bottom right flower. Drape ribbon tails and glue premade ribbon roses over knotted tails.

9. Cut green ombré wire-edge ribbon in three 4" lengths. Refer to General Instructions for Pointed Petal or Leaf on page 15. Fold and stitch each ribbon to form a pointed petal leaf. Glue gathered ends of leaves underneath flowers. Refer to Pewter Frame Placement for location.

10. Using pencil, measure and mark 11" from one end of mauve taffeta ribbon. Beginning at mark, measure three 3" intervals along ribbon, with spaces in-between those intervals of ½" as shown in Diagram B.

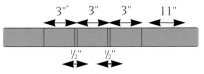

Diagram B

11. Fold ribbon together on first interval marks and gather-stitch, creating a loop, as shown in Diagram C. Secure thread.

Diagram C

12. Repeat for additional two intervals as shown in Diagram D. Wrap remaining ribbon ends around spaces in-between loops.

Diagram D

13. Glue frame to bow, 2" below loops. Refer to General Instructions for Fork Cut on page 12. Fork-cut ribbon ends.

14. Refer to General Instructions for Gathered Rose on page 13. Fold and stitch remaining green/peach /rose ombré wire-edge ribbon to form a gathered rose.

15. Cut remaining green ombré wire-edge ribbon into three 3" lengths. Refer to General Instructions for Pointed Petal or Leaf on page 15. Fold and stitch each ribbon to form a pointed petal leaf.

16. Glue gathered rose and leaves to center of bow.

17. Knot mauve cording into a loop. Glue cording to back of bow to act as a hanger.

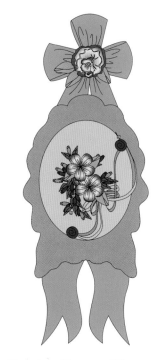

Pewter Frame Placement

Optional Color Combination

Christmas Stocking

Instructions

1. Fold taupe crocheted trim in half, matching cut ends. Using hand-sewing needle and coordinating thread, stitch a narrow seam as shown in Diagram A. Press seam open.

Diagram A

2. Using straight pins, pin taupe crocheted trim around top edge of stocking with seam at center front of stocking. Using large-eyed blunt needle, weave dk. green embroidery ribbon through top edge of crocheted trim while stitching trim onto top edge of stocking.

3. Using hand-sewing needle and coordinating thread, gather-stitch each end of ivory crocheted trim. Tightly gather and secure thread as shown in Diagram B. Position and pin trim underneath bottom edge of taupe crocheted trim, having gathered ends at right side seam of stocking. Using

Materials
Stocking: premade, ivory muslin
Embroidery ribbon: 4mm bronze (¾ yd.), cinnamon (¾ yd.), dk. green (1¾ yds.), dk. rose (1½ yds.), rust (¾ yd.)
Wire-edge ribbon: 1½"-wide, green (⅝ yd.), green metallic ombré (2 yds.)
Trim: 3"-wide taupe crocheted (½ yd.); 5"-wide ivory crocheted (½ yd.)
Pine cones: small (2)

General Supplies & Tools
Glue: craft
Needles: hand-sewing; large-eyed blunt
Scissors: fabric
Sewing machine
Straight pins
Thread: coordinating

sewing machine and a narrow zigzag-stitch, sew trim to stocking.

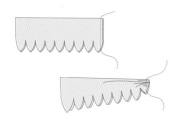

Diagram B

4. Mark green metallic ombré wire-edge ribbon into Pattern A and Pattern B as shown in Diagram C.

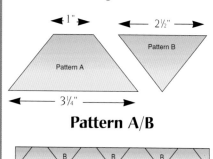

Pattern A/B

Diagram C

5. Using fabric scissors, cut green metallic ombré wire-edge ribbon at markings to yield eighteen A pieces and fifteen B pieces. Set aside B pieces. Gently pull to remove wire from 1"-long edge of each A piece of ribbon. Separate these ribbons into two piles—one with eleven ribbons and one with seven ribbons. From larger pile, gather-stitch ribbon.

6. Refer to General Instructions for Pointed

Petal or Leaf on page 15. Tightly gather to form a petal and secure thread as shown in Diagram D. Without removing thread from first petal, gather-stitch second ribbon. Tightly gather to form a second petal and secure thread.

Diagram D

7. Repeat process, adding another nine petals in the same manner. Join first petal to last and shape flower.

8. Using craft glue, attach flower on top of taupe crocheted trim at top front center edge of stocking.

9. Repeat steps 6–9 using remaining pile of ribbons to form a seven-petal pointed flower. Using craft glue, attach flower on center top of first flower.

10. Return to B pieces of ribbon. Gently pull to remove wire from 2½"-long edge of each B piece of ribbon. Separate ribbons into three piles of five ribbons each.

11. From first pile, gather-stitch first ribbon as shown in Diagram E. Tightly gather to form petal and secure thread. Without removing thread from first petal, gather-stitch second ribbon as shown in Diagram E.

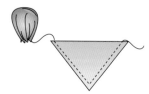

Diagram E

12. Repeat process, adding another three petals in the same manner to form half-bloom as shown in Diagram F.

Diagram F

13. Secure thread. Repeat process for second and third set of five petals. Glue three half-blooms underneath top right side of flower as shown in Christmas Stocking Placement on page 25.

14. Cut dk. rose embroidery ribbon into fifteen 2" lengths. Refer to General Instructions for Knotted Mum on page 13. Join first ribbon to last at seam. Glue knotted mum on top center of flower.

15. Cut green wire-edge ribbon into one 12" length and one 8" length. Refer to General Instructions for Mountain Fold on page 14. Fold 12" ribbon into a triple mountain fold, having each fold 2" deep. Gather-stitch along bottom edge of mountain folds.

16. Tightly gather to form a fan and secure thread. Glue fan underneath left side of flower.

17. Refer to General Instructions for Mountain Fold on page 14. Fold 8" green wire-edge ribbon into double mountain fold, having each fold 2" deep. Gather-stitch along bottom edge of mountain folds.

18. Tightly gather to form fan and secure thread. Glue fan underneath right side of flower.

19. Cut dk. green embroidery ribbon in one 8" length and one 12" length. Fold each ribbon in half. Glue folded center of each ribbon to top of small pine cones. Let glue dry.

20. Tie ribbon ends together and glue underneath lower left side of flower.

21. Hold bronze, cinnamon, rust and remaining dk. rose and dk. green embroidery ribbons together as one. Tie into a 3½"-wide bow. Glue bow underneath left side of flower. Drape ribbon ends and tack in place.

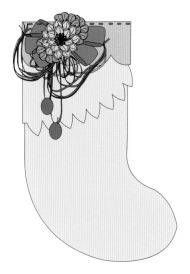

Christmas Stocking Placement

Linen Pillow

Materials
Place mat: white linen, hem-stitched
Embroidery ribbon: 4mm ivory, antique white, pale yellow (1 yd. each)
Sheer ribbon: 1⅜"-wide, white (¾ yd.)
Wire-edge ribbon: ⅞"-wide, pale yellow (1¼ yds.)
Ribbon roses: premade, small, ivory (9)
Blooming roses: premade, ivory grosgrain (5)

General Supplies & Tools
Glue: craft
Iron/ironing board
Needles: hand-sewing
Scissors: fabric
Sewing machine
Stuffing
Thread: coordinating

Instructions
1. Fold one short edge of place mat up 7". Using iron and ironing board, press fold. Machine-stitch side edges together at hem-stitches. Fold remaining short edge of place mat down and press fold. Fill pocket with stuffing. Hand-tack top folded edge along front edge.

2. Refer to General Instructions for Stacked Bow on page 17. Use white sheer ribbon to form stacked bow.

3. Hand-stitch bow to bottom center edge of pillow's top fold as shown on Linen Pillow Placement on page 26. Invisibly hand-tack bow loops to pillow at

8. Glue one blooming rose on top center of each petal. Glue rose/petal on each center of pillow top side at hemstitching.

9. Hold ivory, pale yellow and antique white embroidery ribbons together as one and tie a bow, leaving 7" tails. Glue bow underneath bottom left side of flower cluster.

10. Drape and tack left ribbon tails underneath rose/petal on left side. Knot remaining ribbon ends.

Linen Pillow Placement

Optional Color Combination

random locations to create a tufted appearance.

4. Using fabric scissors, cut pale yellow wire-edge ribbon into three 10" lengths and two 6" lengths. Refer to General Instructions for Circular Ruffle on page 11. Stitch each 10" ribbon to form a circular ruffle.

5. Glue one blooming rose on top center of each circular ruffle as shown in Diagram A.

Diagram A

6. Glue circular ruffles on top center bow in a triangular cluster as shown in Linen Pillow Placement. Glue three sets of three ribbon roses around triangular cluster.

7. Refer to General Instructions for Squared-Off Petal on page 17. Stitch each 6" yellow ribbon to form a squared-off petal.

into 13 mountain folds, having each fold ¾" deep. Tightly gather and join ends together to form petaled flower.

2. Slip petaled flower over bottle cap and pull gathers snug to fit cap. Secure thread. Using industrial-strength adhesive, attach flower to bottle cap.

3. Using fabric scissors, cut lt. lavender sheer ribbon into nine 4" lengths. Refer to General Instructions for Knotted Mum on page 13. Do not join ends. Trim seam to ¼".

4. Glue knotted mum to center back of bottle cap, inside lavender floral flower.

5. Cut lavender wire-edge ribbon into four 10" lengths. Refer to General Instructions for Rosette on page 16. Stitch each ribbon into a rosette.

6. Glue three rosettes to front of cap, laying petaled flower downward and flat. Glue remaining rosette to

Materials

Crystal perfume bottle
  with cap
Embroidery ribbon: 4mm
  olive green, dk. olive green,
  pastel green (¾ yd. each)
Sheer ribbon: ⅜"-wide
  lt. lavender (1 yd.); 1½"-wide
  lavender floral (1 yd.)
Wire-edge ribbon: ⅜"-wide
  lavender (1⅛ yds.); ⅞"-wide
  sage green (¼ yd.)

General Supplies & Tools

Adhesive: industrial-strength
Needles: hand-sewing
Scissors: fabric
Straight pins
Thread: coordinating

Instructions

1. Refer to General Instructions for Mountain Fold on page 14. Using straight pins, fold and pin lavender floral sheer ribbon center back of cap, laying petaled flower upward and flat.

7. Refer to General Instructions for Pointed Petal or Leaf on page 15. Fold and stitch sage green wire-edge ribbon to form three pointed petal leaves.

8. Glue gathered ends of leaves underneath front three rosettes as shown on Front Cap Placement.

9. Remove bottle cap. Hold olive green, dk. olive green and pastel green embroidery ribbons together as one. Tie into bow around bottleneck. Knot ribbon ends.

Front Cap Placement

Back Cap Placement

Crystal Perfume Bottle Placement

Optional Color Placement

Vanity Set

Materials
Vanity mirror, brush, and
    comb set
Embroidery ribbon: 4mm
    ivory, antique white
    (¾ yd. each)
Picot-edge ribbon: ⅝"-wide
    ivory sheer stripe (1¼ yds.)
Sheer ribbon: ⅞"-wide
    antique white stripe (¾ yd.);
    1½"-wide ivory (⅞ yd.)

General Supplies & Tools
Glue: craft
Needles: hand-sewing
Scissors: fabric
Thread: coordinating

Instructions
1. Refer to General Instructions for Stacked Bow on page 17. Hold ivory and antique white embroidery ribbons together as one to form a 12-stacked bow that is 3½" wide.

2. Using craft glue, attach stacked bow to top back of brush handle.

3. Using fabric scissors, cut antique white stripe sheer ribbon in one 12" length. Refer to General Instructions for Circular Ruffle on page 11. Stitch ribbon into a circular ruffle. Set aside.

4. Cut ivory sheer stripe picot-edge ribbon into one 14" length. Refer to General Instructions for Rosette on page 16. Stitch ribbon to form a rosette. Glue rosette on center top of circular ruffle. Glue circular ruffle on top of embroidery ribbon bow on brush.

5. Refer to General Instructions for Stacked Bow on page 17. Fold ivory sheer ribbon back and forth to form a 4-stacked bow that is 4½" wide with 7" tails.

Brush Placement

6. Glue stacked bow to top back of mirror handle. Refer to General Instructions for Fork Cut on page 12. Fork-cut ribbon tails.

7. Cut remaining ivory sheer stripe picot-edge ribbon in half. Refer to General Instructions for Rosette on page 16. Stitch each ribbon to form a rosette. Set aside.

8. Cut remaining antique white stripe sheer ribbon into three 4" lengths to make a bud. Refer to General

Instructions for Gathered Rose on page 13. Follow steps 1, 2, and 3, and continue to roll ribbon creating a bud. Secure with thread. Glue rosettes and buds to center of bow.

Mirror Placement

Bookends

Materials

Wall frames: 5" x 7" decorative wood (2)

Picture insert of choice: (2)

Bookends: 5" x 7" brown metal (1 pair)

Wire-edge ribbon: ⅝"-wide peach (½ yd.); 1½"-wide brown/dusty/peach ombré (1½ yds.), ivory sheer (2 yds.)

Ribbon roses: premade, rust, large (2)

General Supplies & Tools

Glue: craft; industrial-strength

Needles: hand-sewing

Pencil: marking

Scissors: fabric

Straight pins

Thread: coordinating

6. Cut ivory sheer wire-edge ribbon into two equal lengths. With one length, tie bow that is 5½" wide with 7" tails, making a 4-loop bow. Gather-stitch down center of each looped bow. Tightly gather and secure thread. Repeat for second length.

7. Glue one bow behind large flower at center back of each bookend. Secure ribbon tails to side of bookends with glue as shown in Bookend Placement. Shape bow loops as desired.

Bookend Placement

Instructions

1. Insert picture of choice into each decorative wood wall frame. Using industrial-strength glue, attach wall frames to brown metal bookends. Let glue dry.

2. Using fabric scissors, cut brown/dusty peach ombré wire-edge ribbon into two 26½" lengths. Refer to General Instructions for Large Flower on page 13. Using a marking pencil, mark each ribbon with four 5" and one 6½" intervals. Make two large flowers.

3. Fold each flower in half and glue together using craft glue. Glue one flower to top center of each wood frame.

4. Cut peach wire-edge ribbon into two 7" lengths. Refer to General Instructions for Circular Ruffle on page 11. Stitch each ribbon into a circular ruffle.

5. Glue one circular ruffle to center of each large flower. Glue one ribbon rose in center of each circular ruffle.

Instructions

1. Using fabric scissors, cut pink floral print sheer ribbon and pale yellow wire-edge ribbon each into nine 3½" lengths.

2. Using straight pins, layer and pin one pale yellow wire-edge ribbon on top of one pink floral print sheer ribbon. Repeat process for remaining ribbons.

3. Refer to General Instructions for Pointed Petal or Leaf on page 15. Make nine pointed leaves and join leaves together.

4. Refer to General Instructions for Gathered Rose on page 13. With selvage edges matching, fold remaining pink floral print sheer ribbon in half and pin. Stitch to form gathered rose. Glue rose on top center of flower. Using craft glue, attach flower just below middle at center.

5. Cut dk. rose taffeta wire-edge ribbon into three pieces using Pattern A on page 32. Gently pull to remove wire from each 1½"-long edge.

Materials

Pillow: premade,15"-square ivory/rose floral print with ruffles

Sheer ribbon: ⅝"-wide cream (2¾ yds.); 1½"-wide pink floral print (2 yds.)

Wire-edge ribbon: ⅞"-wide lt. pine (1 yd.); brown/dusty peach ombré (1 yd.); 1½"-wide dk. rose taffeta (½ yd.); pale yellow (1⅛ yds.)

Woven ribbon: 1½"-wide, ivory (½ yd.)

Ribbon roses: premade, dk. rose, small (8)

General Supplies & Tools

Fray preventative
Glue: craft
Needles: hand-sewing
Pencil: marking
Scissors: fabric
Straight pins
Thread: coordinating

Gather-stitch each ribbon along edges as shown in Diagram A.

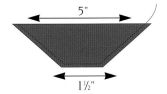

Pattern A/Diagram A

6. Tightly gather and secure thread. Fold ends over to center to form a bud as shown in Diagram B. Secure thread. Repeat process for remaining ribbon pieces.

Diagram B

7. Glue gathered edges of two buds underneath lower right side of flower and gathered edge of one bud underneath top right side of flower.

8. Cut lt. pine wire-edge ribbon in five 7" lengths. Refer to General Instructions for Gathered Leaf on page 13. Fold and stitch each ribbon to form a gathered leaf.

9. Glue gathered edges of four leaves underneath flower and around buds. Set fifth leaf aside.

10. Cut cream sheer ribbon in seven 14" lengths. Refer to General Instructions for Rosette on page 16. Stitch each ribbon to form a rosette.

11. Glue rosettes in a winding fashion, starting at top center of pillow and ending among bottom leaves and buds. Glue gathered edge of remaining leaf underneath one of top rosettes as shown on Floral Pillow Placement.

12. Cut brown/dusty peach ombré wire-edge ribbon in ten equal lengths. Refer to General Instructions for Pointed Petal or Leaf on page 15. Fold and stitch each ribbon to form a pointed petal, alternating light and dark edge outward.

13. Glue leaves underneath rosettes. Randomly glue premade ribbon roses among rosettes.

14. Refer to General Instructions for Mountain Fold on page 14. Using marking pencil, mark 7" from one end of ivory woven ribbon. At mark, fold and pin ribbon into two mountain folds that are 2" deep. Gather-stitch across bottom

edge of folds, not ribbon edge. Tightly gather and secure thread. Leave 7" tail at remaining end of ribbon.

15. Refer to General Instructions for Fork Cut on page 12. Fork-cut ribbon tails. Using fray preventative, following manufacturer's instructions, seal cut ends.

16. Glue mountain folds underneath bottom left side of flower.

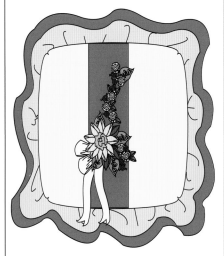

Floral Pillow Placement

Ivory Moiré Box

Materials

Oval box: 20"-diameter,
  covered with ivory moiré
  fabric
Fabric: moiré, lt. peach (⅓ yd.)
Embroidery ribbon: 4mm
  ivory, pastel green
  (1 yd. each)
Satin ribbon: ¼"-wide lt. pine
  (2½ yds.)
Sheer ribbon: 1½"-wide
  peach floral print (2 yds.)
Wire-edge ribbon: ⅞"-wide
  lt. pine (½ yd.)

Woven ribbon: 1½"-wide
  peach moiré taffeta (1 yd.)
Lace: gold delicate (⅓ yd.)
Poster board: 6" x 8"
Quilt batting: ¼ yd.

General Supplies & Tools

Glue: craft
Needles: hand-sewing
Pencil
Scissors: craft; fabric
Straight pins
Thread: coordinating

Instructions

1. Using pencil, trace box
lid onto poster board. Using
craft scissors, cut out
traced lid.

2. Trace poster board lid
onto wrong side of lt. peach
fabric and gold lace, ¾"
larger than lid. Using craft
glue, glue quilt batting to
poster board. Using fabric
scissors, trim batting flush to
poster board's edge, slightly
beveling quilt batting
inward. Center and snugly
wrap fabric and lace to back
of poster board. Trim all bulk
and secure fabric and lace to
poster board with glue.

3. Using fabric scissors, cut
lt. pine satin ribbon in one
21" length. Using thin layer
of craft glue, snugly attach
ribbon to bottom edge of
box. Overlap ribbon at center
back and glue in place.

4. Cut peach floral print
sheer ribbon into one 21"
length. Snugly wrap ribbon
around top of box lid. Glue
ribbon to lid at back center
only so that glue will not
show through ribbon. Wrap
upper edge of ribbon over

top of box and secure in place with glue.

5. Refer to General Instructions for Fluting on page 12. Flute while gluing lt. pine satin ribbon to inside edge of padded box lid. Glue padded lid to box top, making certain peach floral print sheer ribbon is tucked down and lt. pine satin flutes are pointed up.

6. Cut peach moiré taffeta ribbon in three 6" lengths. Refer to General Instructions for Squared-Off Petal on page 17. Using hand-sewing needle and coordinating thread, stitch each ribbon to form a squared-off petal. Glue petals on center of padded lid.

7. Cut peach floral print sheer ribbon into three 8" lengths. Refer to General Instructions for Squared-Off Petal on page 17. Stitch each ribbon to form a squared-off petal. Tightly gather and secure thread. Glue petals on top of peach taffeta petals.

8. Cut peach moiré taffeta ribbon and peach floral print sheer ribbon each into three 6" lengths. Using straight pins, layer and pin one sheer ribbon over one solid ribbon.

Repeat process for remaining ribbons.

9. Fold one set of layered ribbons in half to mark center. Fold one cut edge down ¼". Fold opposite edge over ¼" past center mark. Fold the folded down edge over to meet center mark as shown in Diagram A. Pin to hold.

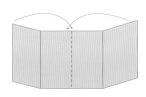

Diagram A

Gather-stitch as shown in Diagram B.

Diagram B

Tightly gather to form flower and secure thread as shown in Diagram C.

Diagram C

10. Repeat process for remaining two layered ribbons. Glue flowers, with points facing upward, on top center of taffeta/sheer petals.

11. Cut lt. pine wire-edge ribbon into two 7" lengths. Refer to General Instructions for Gathered Leaf on page 13. Make a gathered leaf pulling gathers so that ribbon measures 1".

12. Repeat process for remaining ribbon. Glue leaves underneath top right side of peach petals.

13. Refer to General Instructions for Stacked Bow on page 17. Hold ivory and pastel green embroidery ribbons together as one and form a stacked bow that is 3½"-wide with 7" tails.

14. Knot ends of ribbon tails. Glue stacked bow in-between left side of sheer and taffeta petals.

Ivory Moiré Box Placement

Miniature Violin

Materials

Miniature wooden violin
  and bow
Embroidery ribbon: 4mm
  gold (¾ yd.), olive green
  (⅜ yd.), dk. rose (⅜ yd.)
Velvet ribbon: ³⁄₁₆"-wide
  green (⅝ yd.)
Wire-edge ribbon: ⅞"-wide
  burgundy/mauve ombré
  (1 yd.); 1½"-wide burgundy
  (1¼ yd.), green (1½ yd.)
Filigrees: antique brass (5)

General Supplies & Tools

Glue: craft
Adhesive: industrial-strength
Needles: hand-sewing
Pencil: marking
Pliers: needlenose
Scissors: fabric
Straight pins
Thread: coordinating

Instructions

1. Using fabric scissors, cut
green wire-edge ribbon into
one 44" length. Refer to
General Instructions for
Stacked Bow on page 17.
Form a stacked bow that is
5½" wide with 5" tails.

2. Using craft glue, attach
stacked bow to back of
violin neck.

3. Refer to General
Instructions for Fork Cut on
page 12. Fork-cut ribbon tails.

4. Cut burgundy wire-edge
ribbon in one 30" length.
Refer to General Instructions
for Stacked Bow on page 17.
Form a stacked bow that is
4" wide with one 7" tail and
one 10" tail. Glue bow to top
of violin neck, in front of
green bow.

5. Refer to General
Instructions for Fork Cut on
page 12. Fork-cut ribbon
tails.

6. Cut burgundy/mauve
ombré wire-edge ribbon into
three 10½" lengths. Refer to
General Instructions for
Pansy on page 15. Make
three pansies.

7. Cut gold embroidery ribbon into three 9" lengths. Tie each ribbon into a small bow. Trim ends short.

8. Glue one bow to each pansy center. Glue two of the pansies on top of burgundy bow. Set third pansy aside.

9. Cut green velvet ribbon into five 3½" lengths. Refer to General Instructions for Knotted Mum on page 13. Make five petals. Do not join first to last.

10. Glue knotted mums to burgundy bow, beneath top left side of pansies.

11. Hold olive green and dk. rose embroidery ribbons together as one and tie into a 2½"-wide bow at center of ribbons.

12. Glue bow to burgundy bow, underneath lower left side of pansies.

13. Using industrial-strength adhesive, glue two filigrees on top of violin neck, one slightly above burgundy bow and one slightly below burgundy bow.

14. Using needlenose pliers, bend remaining three filigrees. Glue two filigrees to burgundy bow, one slightly beneath green velvet bow and one slightly beneath top right side of pansy.

15. Refer to General Instructions for Mountain Fold on page 13. Fold remaining green wire-edge ribbon into a triple mountain fold, having each fold 1¼" deep. With folds facing downward, glue ribbon to front top of violin bow.

16. Using craft glue, glue remaining pansy over stitched edge of green wire-edge ribbon.

17. Tie remaining burgundy wire-edge ribbon into 3"-wide bow with 3" tails. Refer to General Instructions for Fork Cut on page 12. Fork-cut bow tails.

18. Glue to violin bow, underneath top of pansy. Using industrial-strength adhesive, glue remaining antique brass filigree to flower, underneath left side.

Miniature Violin Placement

Miniature Violin Bow Placement

Porcelain Box

Instructions

1. Fit white embroidered fabric onto lid of porcelain box.

2. Using marking pencil and beginning and ending with a ¼"-mark, mark lavender wire-edge ribbon so there are seven ¾" intervals on one edge and six ¾" intervals on the other edge as shown on Diagram A.

Using hand-sewing needle and coordinating thread, gather-stitch in a zigzag as shown in Diagram A. Tightly gather and secure thread. Shape petals to cup downward.

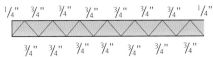

Diagram A

3. Using fabric scissors, cut pale yellow wire-edge ribbon into five 1½" lengths. Refer to General Instructions for Gathered Rose, steps 1, 2, and 3 on page 13. Stitch each ribbon into a gathered rosebud.

4. Cut coral wire-edge

Materials

Porcelain box: with lid suitable for covering
Embroidered fabric: 4½"-square, white
Embroidery ribbon: 4mm soft blush (½ yd.), pastel green (½ yd.), lt. orchid (1⅓ yds.)
Sheer ribbon: 1½"-wide, white (½ yd.)
Wire-edge ribbon: ⅜"-wide coral (⅜ yd.); ⅝"-wide lavender, pale yellow (¼ yd. each)
Ribbon roses: premade, small, dk. mauve (3)

General Supplies & Tools

Glue: craft
Needles: hand-sewing
Pencil: marking
Scissors: fabric
Straight pins
Thread: coordinating

ribbon into three 4" lengths. Using Pattern A circle, trace three half-circles onto each ribbon, leaving ¼" on each side of first and last half circles as shown in Diagram B.

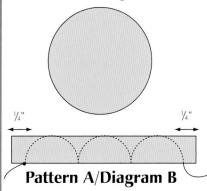

Pattern A/Diagram B

5. Gather-stitch along traced circles. Tightly gather to form petals and secure thread. Keep petals from twisting to opposite sides. Join first petal to last at seam. Secure thread. Cup petals downward.

6. Cut lt. orchid embroidery ribbon into six 5" lengths. Refer to General Instructions for Rosette on page 16. Stitch each ribbon into rosette.

7. Position rosettes, and ribbon roses, on lid. Attach to lid using craft glue.

8. Refer to General Instructions for Mountain Fold on page 14. Using straight pins, fold and pin white sheer ribbon into four mountain folds.

9. Glue gathered edge behind floral arrangement.

10. Hold soft blush, pastel green and remaining lt. orchid embroidery ribbons together as one and tie in a 2½"-wide bow with 5" tails. Knot tail ends.

11. Glue to lid in between floral arrangement and sheer bow. Drape and secure ribbon ends to lid with craft glue.

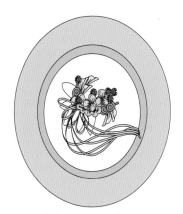

Porcelain Box Placement

Mini Chair

Materials

Iron chair: miniature
Ribbon roses: premade, small, lt. lavender (2), dk. mauve (3)
Wired ribbon, ¾"-wide: black floral-print (1 yd.)
Wire-edge ribbon: ⅞"-wide olive green ombré (2¼ yds.); 1½"-wide green (⅜ yd.)

General Supplies & Tools

Glue: craft
Needles: hand-sewing
Pencil: marking
Ruler
Scissors: fabric
Straight pins
Thread: coordinating

Instructions

1. Refer to General Instructions for Mountain Fold on page 14. Using ruler and marking pencil, measure and mark 7" from left end of olive green ombré wire-edge ribbon. Beginning at mark and using straight pins, fold and pin five mountain folds that are ¾" deep. Tightly gather to form fan and secure thread, but do not cut ribbon.

2. Measure and mark a 3½" space from end of gathered mountain folds. Beginning at mark, fold and pin three mountain folds as in step 1 that are ¾" deep as shown in Diagram A. Gather-stitch as in step 1. Do not cut ribbon.

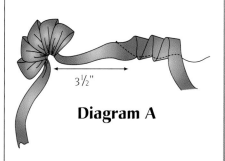

3½"

Diagram A

Pointed Petal or Leaf on page 15. Form five sets of pointed petal leaves with two petals in each set as shown in Diagram B.

Diagram B

8. Using craft glue, attach each pair of leaves in front of each set of olive green mountain folds. Glue ribbon roses on top center of petal leaves, alternating colors.

9. Gather-stitch along one selvage edge of green wire-edge ribbon. Tightly gather to form fan and secure thread. Using craft glue, attach ribbon fan to back of top center ribbons shown as in Diagram C.

Diagram C

3. Measure and mark a 3½" space from end of gathered mountain folds from the second set. Beginning at mark, fold and pin five mountain folds that are ¾" deep.

4. Measure and mark a 3½" space from end of third set of mountain folds. Beginning at mark, fold and pin three mountain folds that are ¾" deep. Gather-stitch as in step 1. Do not cut ribbon.

5. Measure and mark a 3½" space from end of gathered mountain folds from the fourth set. Beginning at mark, fold and pin five mountain folds that are ¾" deep.

6. Refer to General Instructions for Fork Cut on page 12. Fork-cut ribbon tails. Evenly drape and stitch ribbon cascade to back of chair as shown on Mini Chair Placement.

7. Using fabric scissors, cut black floral print ribbon into five equal lengths. Refer to General Instructions for

Mini Chair Placement

Bear's Outfit

Materials

Plush bear: 12"
Embroidery ribbon: 4mm
green (¼ yd.)
Wire-edge ribbon: ⅞"-wide
green ombré (⅓ yd.);
2¼"-wide floral print (1¾ yds.)
Ribbon roses: premade, small,
lt. lavender (2), mauve (2)
Doll hat: small, mauve, woven

General Supplies & Tools

Glue: craft
Iron/ironing board
Needles: hand-sewing
Scissors: fabric
Sewing machine
Thread: coordinating

Instructions

1. Using fabric scissors, cut floral print wire-edge ribbon into one 6" length, one 8" length, one 20" length, and one 28" length.

2. Gently pull wires to remove them from both edges of 6" ribbon and from one edge of 20" and 28" ribbons. Knot and secure remaining wire at one end of 20" and 28" ribbons. Pull wire to gather ribbons.

3. Using sewing machine, sew 20" gathered ribbon to one edge of 6" ribbon. Sew 28" gathered ribbon to remaining edge of 20" ribbon to form bodice and layered skirt. With right sides together, sew raw edges of bodice together.

4. Place bear in bodice and skirt. Fold top edge of bodice under ¼" and hem.

5. Fit bodice to bear by turning raw edges of ribbon inward accordingly. Using hand-sewing needle and coordinating thread, stitch bodice where needed.

6. Sew long edges of 8" ribbon together. Position seam in center of ribbon. Press ribbon with iron.

7. Tuck one end of ribbon into bodice. Wrap ribbon around neck of bear and tuck remaining end of ribbon into bodice to form V-neck line. Tack ribbons to bodice. Sew one mauve ribbon rose over tack.

8. Refer to General Instructions for Fork Cut on page 12. Gently pull wires to remove them from both edges of green ombré wire-edge ribbon. Tie ribbon around waist. Fork-cut ribbon ends.

9. Using craft glue, wrap and glue green embroidery ribbon around hat to form a hat band, leaving ribbon tails to overlap as shown in Bear's Outfit Placement.

10. Glue remaining ribbon roses to hat band at overlap.

11. Place bear in iron chair. Place hat on bear's lap or on head as desired.

Bear's Outfit Placement

Lace Shoes

Fold on page 14. Fold each ribbon into two mountain folds that are 2½" deep. Using hand-sewing needle and coordinating thread, gather-stitch along bottom edge of mountain folds. Tightly gather and secure thread.

2. Using craft glue, attach two ribbon loops to each dress shoe, ½" from top center as shown in Diagram A.

Diagram A

3. Glue three swirl roses to top center of each dress shoe.

4. Glue one petal rose underneath each swirl rose, pushing the top petals downward to form a half-bloom as shown in Diagram B.

Diagram B

Materials
Dress shoes: ivory lace
Picot-edge ribbon: ⅝"-wide ivory sheer stripe (1⅛ yds.)
Wire-edge ribbon: ⅝"-wide cream (¾ yd.); 1½"-wide pale yellow polka dot (1¼ yds.)
Petal roses: ivory (2)
Swirl roses: ivory, miniature (6)

General Supplies & Tools
Glue: craft
Needles: hand-sewing
Scissors: fabric
Thread: coordinating

Instructions
1. Using fabric scissors, cut pale yellow polka dot wire-edge ribbon into four 10½" lengths. Refer to General Instructions for Mountain

5. Cut cream wire-edge ribbon into two 12" lengths. Refer to General Instructions for Squared-Off Petal on page 17. Make each ribbon into a squared-off petal.

6. Tightly wrap each squared-off petal above each rose cluster as shown in Diagram C.

Diagram C

7. Glue gathered ends, evenly positioned, beneath each rose cluster.

8. Cut ivory sheer stripe picot-edge ribbon into two 20" lengths. Refer to General Instructions for Squared-Off Petal on page 17. Gather-stitch each ribbon to form a squared-off petal.

9. Tightly wrap each squared-off petal below each rose cluster and above ribbon loops as shown in Diagram D. Glue gathered ends, evenly positioned, beneath each rose cluster.

Diagram D

10. Allow the shoe embellishments to dry before wearing shoes.

Lace Shoe Placement

Lace Shoes Optional Color Combination
Materials
Dress shoes: black linen
Picot-edge ribbon: ⅝"-wide gray (1⅛ yds.)
Wire-edge ribbon: ⅝"-wide red (¾ yd.); 1½"-wide dk. green (1¼ yds.)
Petal roses: white (2)
Swirl roses: white, miniature (6)

General Supplies & Tools
Glue: craft
Needles: hand-sewing
Scissors: fabric
Thread: coordinating

Instructions
Follow instructions for Lace Shoes. Substitute original materials with those outlined in Materials and General Supplies & Tools lists.

Diagram A

Diagram B

Diagram C

Diagram D

Lace Shoe Placement

Gift Gazebo

into one 36½" length. Refer to General Instructions for Large Flower on page 13. Using marking pencil, mark ribbon with six 5" and one 6½" intervals. Make ribbon into a large flower.

2. Place large flower on top of gazebo and gather until flower fits 2" below top of gazebo. Stitch ribbon flower to gazebo to hold in place.

3. Cut fruit-print wire-edge ribbon into one 30½" length. Mark ribbon with five 5" and one 6½" intervals. Make ribbon into a large flower.

4. Place ribbon flower on top of gazebo and gather until flower fits on top of first ribbon flower. Stitch ribbon flower to gazebo to hold in place.

5. Cut brown/dusty peach ombré wire-edge ribbon into one 26½" length. Mark ribbon with four 5" and one 6½" intervals. Make ribbon into a large flower.

6. Place flower on top of gazebo and gather until

Materials
Wrought-iron gazebo
Sheer ribbon: ⅝"-wide pink azalea with gold-edge (1¾ yds.)
Embroidery ribbon: 4mm bronze, burgundy, olive green, lt. olive green, mauve (⅝ yd. each)
Wire-edge ribbon: 1½"-wide brown/dusty peach ombré (¾ yd.), fruit-print (1⅞ yds.), purple ombré (1½ yds.)

General Supplies & Tools
Needles: hand-sewing
Pencil: marking
Scissors: fabric
Straight pins
Thread: coordinating

Instructions
1. Using fabric scissors, cut fruit-print wire-edge ribbon

flower fits on top of second ribbon flower. Stitch ribbon flower to gazebo to hold in place.

7. Cut pink azalea sheer ribbon into one 36" and one 27" length. Refer to General Instructions for Circular Ruffle on page 11. Make each ribbon into a circular ruffle.

8. Place large circular ruffle on top of third ribbon flower. Stitch circular ruffle to gazebo to hold in place. Repeat process for small circular ruffle.

9. Refer to Stacked Bow on page 17. Fold purple wire-edge ribbon to form a Stacked Bow with 9" tails. Stitch bow to gazebo, just below first ribbon flower, to hold in place.

10. Refer to General Instructions for Fork Cut on page 12. Fork-cut ribbon ends.

11. Hold all embroidery ribbons together as one and knot one set of ribbon ends. Make one 6" loop and stitch end of loop to knotted end to hold in place. Drape loose ends downward. Knot ribbon tails. Stitch to top of bow.

12. Fill with desired gift or items.

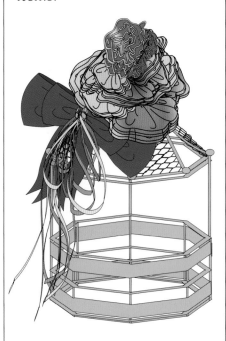

Gift Gazebo Placement

Kissing Ball

Materials

Ornament: 13" silver ball
Metallic ribbon: ¼"-wide silver (1¾ yds.); ⅞" metallic ribbon (⅛ yd)
Wire-edge ribbon: 1½"-wide pink metallic ombré (1¾ yds.); 2¼"-wide pink/green plaid (1⅛ yds); ⅞"-wide pink ombré (1½ yds.)
Beads: silver
Mistletoe: 1 package
Tassel: silver

General Supplies & Tools

Glue: craft
Needles: embroidery; hand-sewing
Scissors: fabric
Thread: coordinating; transparent (¼ yd.)

Instructions

1. Fill ornament with mistletoe.

2. Use wire-edged pink ombré ribbon to package-wrap around ornament. Refer to Kissing Ball Placement on page 45.

3. Refer to General Instructions for Mountain Fold on page 14. Fold pink/green plaid wire-edge ribbon into six mountain folds, having each fold 3" deep. Using hand-sewing needle and coordinating thread, gather-stitch along edge with cut ends. Shape into a flower.

4. Using craft glue, attach flower to top of ornament so that folds do not meet at center front.

5. Using fabric scissors and pattern provided, cut pink metallic ombré wire-edge ribbon into 10 equal lengths of Pattern A on page 45.

edge ribbons into pointed petals. Join first petal to last and shape into a flower. Glue flower on center top of pink metallic ombré flower.

9. Cut silver metallic ribbon into fifteen 3" lengths. Refer to General Instructions for Knotted Mum on page 13. Make ribbons into knotted mums.

10. Glue knotted mum on center top of flower.

11. Using embroidery needle and ⅞" metallic ribbon. Thread ribbon though bottom center of ornament. Run needle through beads and attach tassel to end with needle. Knot to secure.

12. Loop transparent thread through top of ornament and knot for hanger.

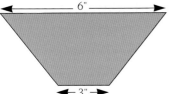

Pattern A

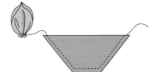

Diagram A

6. Refer to General Instructions for Pointed Petal or Leaf on page 15. Remove wire from 3"-long edge of each cut ribbon. Without removing thread from first petal, gather-stitch second ribbon as shown in Diagram A. Tightly gather to form a second petal and secure thread.

7. Repeat process, adding the remaining five petals. Join first petal to last and shape into a flower. Glue flower on top of pink/green plaid flower made in step 3.

8. Refer to General Instructions for Pointed Petal or Leaf on page 5. Make the remaining three pink metallic ombré wire-

Kissing Ball Placement

Marinda Stewart

Marinda Stewart's work has appeared in countless books and magazines in a career that spans more than 20 years. She is the author of four specialty books along with her own line of patterns for clothing and accessories. Marinda has demonstrated various needlework techniques and her projects have been on television and in instructional videos.

Marinda's imaginative use of fabrics and trims along with her design sense, combines to produce consistently interesting and popular projects. She has coordinated for many wearable art fashion shows and acted as commentator. Several celebrities are counted among the people who own her wearable art while a number of other pieces are in corporate collections.

Box

Materials

Box: 5" square, covered in
   mauve moiré fabric
Wire-edge ribbon: 1½"-wide
   gold mesh (1¾ yds.),
   green/pink metallic ombré
   (⅞ yd.), sage taffeta (½ yd.)
Trim: ¾"-wide metallic gold
   (½ yd.)
Beads: miniature pearl (3)
Cotton ball

General Supplies & Tools

Hot glue gun and glue sticks
Needles: hand-sewing
Scissors: fabric
Thread: coordinating

Instructions

1. Using fabric scissors, cut
gold mesh wire-edge ribbon
into two 8½" lengths and two
14" lengths. Wrap ribbons
around box lid and box
bottom as shown on
Diagram A. Using hot glue
gun and glue stick, attach
ribbon ends to inside of box
lid and box bottom.

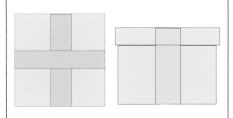

Diagram A

2. Glue metallic gold trim
in a circle on top of box lid.

3. Cut remaining gold mesh
wire-edge ribbon into six 3"
lengths. Refer to General
Instructions for Pointed
Petal or Leaf on page 15.
Make each ribbon into a
pointed leaf.

4. Cut sage wire-edge
ribbon into six 3" lengths.
Make each ribbon into a
pointed leaf.

5. Evenly space and glue gold mesh leaves on top of box lid, inside gold trim circle. Glue sage green leaves on top and between gold mesh leaves as shown in Diagram B.

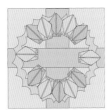

Diagram B

6. Cut green/pink metallic ombré wire-edge ribbon into one 4" length. Refer to General Instructions for Seed Pod on page 17. Make one seed pod. Glue miniature pearl beads over pink gathered edge.

7. Refer to General Instructions for Stitched Flower on page 17. Use 5" of remaining green/pink metallic ombré ribbon to make one five-petal stitched flower, marking five intervals spaced 1" apart.

8. Glue bottom of seed pod to center of stitched flower. Glue bottom of stitched flower to top of leaves. Refer to Box Placement.

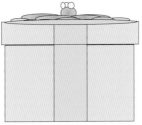

Box Placement

Pen

Materials
Wire-edge ribbon : ⅜"-wide sage taffeta (½ yd.); 1½"-wide green/pink metallic ombré (⅝ yd.), sage taffeta (¼ yd.)
Embroidery ribbon: 4mm mauve (½ yd.)
Leaf: velvet
Cotton ball
Pen: ballpoint

General Supplies & Tools
Hot glue gun and glue sticks
Needles: embroidery; hand-sewing
Scissors: fabric
Thread: coordinating

Instructions
1. Using ⅜"-wide sage wire-edge ribbon, tightly wrap pen. Fold any raw edges under. Secure ends with a dab of hot glue.

2. Using fabric scissors, cut 1½"-wide sage wire-edge ribbon into two equal lengths. Refer to General Instructions for Pointed Petal or Leaf on page 15. Fold and stitch each ribbon into a pointed leaf.

3. Cut green/pink metallic ombré ribbon into one 4" length. Refer to General Instructions for Seed Pod on page 17. Make each ribbon into a seed pod.

4. Refer to Spider Web Rose on page 50. Using embroidery needle and mauve embroidery ribbon, stitch a spider web rose on top of seed pod.

5. Refer to General Instructions for Stitched Flower on page 17. Use 3" of green/pink metallic ombré ribbon to make one five-petal stitched flower, marking five intervals spaced ½" apart.

6. Glue seed pod, with rose side up, in center of stitched flower.

7. Cut small slit in center of velvet leaf. Slip leaf over top of pen and secure with a dab of glue. Glue pointed leaves to bottom of velvet leaf as shown in Diagram A on page 49. Glue stitched flower to velvet leaf.

Diagram A

Pen Placement

Note Card

Materials

Note card: 5" x 5" with
   scalloped edges
Cardstock: 3½" x 3½" tan
Sheer ribbon: ½"-wide peach
   (⅝ yd.)
Wire-edge ribbon: ⅜"-wide
   sage taffeta (⅛ yd.); 1½"-
   wide green/pink metallic
   ombré (⅜ yd.), sage taffeta
   (½ yd.)
Ribbon rose: premade,
   small, mauve (1)

General Supplies & Tools

Hot glue gun and glue sticks
Needles: hand-sewing
Scissors: fabric; pinking
   shears
Thread: coordinating

Instructions

1. Using pinking shears, cut edges of tan cardstock paper.

2. Using fabric scissors, cut peach sheer ribbon into four equal lengths. Wrap each ribbon around edges of tan cardstock paper creating a frame. Refer to Note Card Placement. Using hot glue gun and glue stick, secure ribbons to underside of paper with a dab of hot glue.

3. Diagonally center paper and glue to top of note card.

4. Using 3" of 1½"-wide sage wire-edge ribbon, refer to General Instructions for Stitched Flower on page 17. Make one five-petal stitched flower, marking five intervals spaced ½" apart.

5. Using 2½" of green/pink metallic ombré wire-edge ribbon, make one five-petal stitched flower, marking five intervals spaced ½" apart.

6. Glue bottom of green/pink flower on top of sage flower, with petals between each other as shown in Note Card Placement.

7. Gently pull to remove wire from one edge of ⅜"-wide sage wire-edge ribbon. Gather-stitch edge. Tightly gather into a circle and tack

ends together. Glue to center of green/pink flower.

8. Glue premade mauve ribbon rose to center of flower as shown on Note Card Placement.

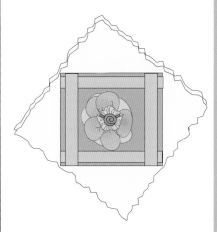

Note Card Placement

Spider Web Rose

1. Using two strands of floss, securely work Straight Stitches to form five spokes as shown on page 50. These are anchor stitches to create web with ribbon.

2. Bring ribbon up through center of spokes.

3. Weave ribbon over one spoke.

4. Weave under next spoke; continue weaving over then under, in one direction until spokes are covered.

5. Completed Spider Web Rose.

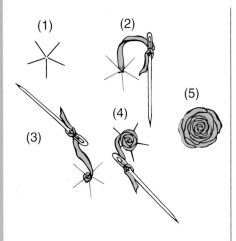

(1) (2)

(3) (4) (5)

Sachet

Materials
Wire-edge ribbon: 1½"-wide
   olive green ombré (½ yd.);
   2¼"-wide peach (1 yd.)
Netting: peach (¼ yd.)
Potpourri beads

General Supplies & Tools
Hot glue gun and glue sticks
Needles: hand-sewing
Thread: coordinating
Scissors: fabric

Instructions
1. Refer to General
Instructions for Rose on
page 16. Using peach wire-
edge ribbon, make a rose.

2. Using fabric scissors, cut
peach netting into a 4"-
diameter circle. Using
hand-sewing needle and

coordinating thread, gather-
stitch around netting. Place
potpourri on netting. Gather
netting around potpourri
to form scented stamen. Sew
stamen to center of rose.

3. Cut olive green ombré
wire-edge ribbon into two
equal lengths. Refer to
General Instructions for Pulled
Petal or Leaf on page 15. Pull
wire on opposite edges of
each ribbon to form one
light leaf and one dark leaf.

4. Using hot glue gun and
glue stick, glue leaves to
back of rose.

Sachet Placement

Wire cutters

Instructions

1. Using fabric scissors, cut sage wire-edge ribbon into sixteen 3" lengths and twelve 4" lengths. Refer to General Instructions for Pointed Petal or Leaf on page 15. Make each 3" length into a pointed petal leaf. Use No-Sew Variation for 4" lengths of ribbon.

2. Using wire cutters, cut florist wire into twelve 5" lengths. Using pale green florist tape and florist wires, wrap 4" No-Sew Variation leaves in clusters of three.

3. Cut dusty pink wire-edge ribbon into two 12" lengths, three 18" lengths, and two 24" lengths. Refer to General Instructions for Rose on page 16. Make each ribbon into a rose, using Crinkled Rose Variation to finish.

4. Cut remaining dusty pink ribbon into six 7" lengths. Refer to General Instructions for Twisted Rosebuds on page 18. Make each ribbon into a twisted rosebud.

Materials

Lamp: 24" with brocade shade and gold base

Sheer ribbon: ⅞"-wide pale pink/gold-edge chiffon (2 yds.); 1½"-wide pale pink/gold-edge (5¼ yds.)

Wire-edge ribbon: 1½"-wide sage taffeta (3⅛ yds.), dusty pink taffeta (5 yds.)

Florist tape: pale green

Florist wire: 16-18 gauge

General Supplies & Tools

Hot glue gun and glue sticks

Needles: hand-sewing

Scissors: fabric

Thread: coordinating

5. Measure circumference of lampshade at bottom. Triple the measurement. Cut pale pink/gold sheer ribbon to length. Sew a gather-stitch down center of ribbon. Gather ribbon to fit base of lampshade. Repeat for top of lampshade.

6. Using hot glue gun and glue stick, attach ribbon to lampshade. Repeat process for top of lampshade.

7. Glue one 18" rose, two 24" roses, pointed leaves and rosebuds to lampshade as shown on Diagram A.

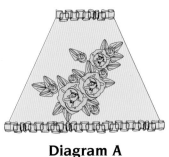

Diagram A

8. Cut florist wire into four 7" lengths.

9. Cut remaining sage green ribbon into four equal lengths. Refer to General Instructions for Calyx on page 11. Attach roses to stem wire. Finish underside of each rose with a calyx.

10. Wrap roses and leaf clusters together with pale green florist tape.

11. Cut ⅞"-wide pale pink/gold-edge sheer ribbon into one 54" length. Refer to General Instructions for Multi-Loop Bow on page 14. Make one multi-loop bow. Tie bow to rose arrangement as shown in Diagram B.

Diagram B

12. Refer to General Instructions for Fork Cut on page 12. Fork-cut ribbon ends.

13. With remaining 18" pale pink/gold wire-edge sheer ribbon, tie rose arrangement to lamp base. Trim excess florist wire as desired. Shape as desired.

Brocade Lamp Placement

Brocade Pillow

Materials
Flanged pillow: 15" x 11" pale green brocade
Sheer ribbon: 1½"-wide moss green chiffon (1⅜ yd.)
Wire-edge ribbon: ⅜"-wide sage taffeta (¼ yd.); ⅝"-wide ivory satin (½ yd.); ⅞"-wide gold mesh (⅞ yd.); 1½"-wide ivory taffeta (½ yd.), sage taffeta (1 yd.), mauve taffeta (1⅛ yds.), yellow taffeta (1¼ yds.)
Trim: metallic gold (1¼ yds.)
Pearls: 7-8 mm (7)
Florist tape: pale green
Florist wire: 16-18 gauge

General Supplies & Tools
Hot glue gun and glue sticks
Needles: hand-sewing
Pencil
Scissors: fabric
Thread: coordinating
Wire cutters

Instructions
1. Refer to General Instructions for Rose on page 16. Using 1½" ivory taffeta wire-edge ribbon,

ribbon into one 18" length and three 7" lengths. Refer to General Instructions for Rose on page 16. Make 18" ribbon into a rose.

6. Refer to General Instructions for Twisted Rosebud on page 18. Fold each 7" ribbon into a twisted rosebud.

7. Cut 1½" sage wire-edge ribbon into twelve 3" lengths. Refer to General Instructions for Pointed Petal or Leaf on page 15. Make each ribbon into a pointed leaf.

8. Cut gold mesh wire-edge ribbon into eleven 2½" lengths. Make each ribbon into a pointed leaf, using No-Sew Variation.

9. Using wire cutters, cut florist wire into two 8" lengths. Using pale green florist tape, wrap leaves in one stem of five and one stem of six.

10. Sew gold metallic trim onto pillow at flange seam.

11. Using hot glue gun and glue stick, *attach flowers, leaves, leaf clusters, and pearls onto pillow top. Refer to Brocade Pillow Placement on page 54.

make one rose, using Antique Rose Variation on page 16.

2. Using fabric scissors, cut ivory satin wire-edge ribbon into three 6" lengths. Refer to General Instructions for Twisted Rosebud on page 18. Make each ribbon into a twisted rosebud.

3. Cut mauve wire-edge ribbon into one 24" length and two 7" lengths. Refer to General Instructions for Rose on page 16. Make 24" ribbon, using Crinkled Rose Variation on page 16.

4. Refer to General Instructions for Twisted Rosebud on page 18. Fold each 7" ribbon into a twisted rosebud.

5. Cut yellow wire-edge

12. Cut moss green sheer ribbon into one 12" length and one 10" length. Loosely knot middle and one end of 12" ribbon. Knot one end of 10" ribbon. Glue onto pillow top. Refer to Brocade Pillow Placement.

13. Refer to General Instructions for Fork Cut on page 12. Fork-Cut knotted ribbon ends.

14. Make four loops from remaining moss green sheer ribbon. Glue between leaves around mauve rose as shown in Diagram A.

Diagram A

15. Tightly twist ⅜"-wide sage wire-edge ribbon into a cord. Twist cord around a pencil to form a tendril. Refer to Diagram B.

Diagram B

16. Glue tendril onto pillow top at base of one leaf cluster as shown on Brocade Pillow Placement.

*All flowers may be stitched onto pillow if desired.

Brocade Pillow Placement

Rose Frame

Materials
Frame: 8" x 10" as desired
Photo mat: 8" x 10" precut oval, sage
Sheer ribbon: ⅞"-wide pale pink/gold-edge (1 yd.)
Wire-edge ribbon: 1½"-wide sage taffeta (2 yds.), dusty pink taffeta (3½ yds.)
Fabric: coordinating small print (¼ yd.)
Florist tape: pale green
Florist wire: 16-18 gauge

General Supplies & Tools
Hot glue gun and glue sticks
Pencil
Scissors: fabric
Thread: coordinating
Wire cutters

Instructions
1. Using pencil, trace pre-cut oval photo mat opening onto wrong side of small print fabric. Using fabric scissors and decreasing opening size by ½", cut out opening. Clip curves.

2. Using hot glue gun and glue stick, attach fabric to mat by folding and gluing fabric edges to back of mat. Insert covered mat into frame.

3. Using wire cutters, cut florist wire into four 12" lengths and five 9" lengths. Set aside.

4. Cut sage wire-edge ribbon into seventeen 4" lengths. Set aside five ribbons. Refer to General Instructions for Pointed Petal or Leaf on page 15. Make twelve ribbons into a pointed leaf, using No-Sew Variation on page 15.

10. Refer to General Instructions for Fork Cut on page 12. Fork-cut ribbon ends.

11. Arrange and glue roses, rosebuds, leaf clusters, and bow on left side of frame as shown on Rose Frame Placement.

Rose Frame Placement

5. Using pale green florist tape, wrap leaves in clusters of three on florist wire. Make four clusters.

6. Cut dusty pink wire-edge ribbon into two 24" lengths and three 12" lengths. Refer to General Instructions for Rose on page 16. Make each ribbon into a rose, using Crinkled Rose Variation on page 16.

7. Refer to General Instructions for Calyx on page 11. Using 9" wires, attach roses and use five remaining 4" sage ribbons to make calyxes.

8. Cut remaining dusty pink wire-edge ribbon into five 8" lengths. Refer to General Instructions for Twisted Rosebud on page 18. Make each ribbon into a twisted rosebud.

9. Refer to General Instructions for Multi-Loop Bow on page 14. Using pale pink/gold-edge sheer ribbon, make a multi-loop bow.

Satin Cap

Materials
Baseball cap: ivory satin, quilted
Sheer ribbon, 1½"-wide: peach organdy/satin striped (1 yd.)
Wire-edge ribbon: ⅜"-wide sage taffeta (1 yd.); 1½"-wide dk. peach taffeta (½ yd.); 2¼"-wide peach (1½ yds.)

General Supplies & Tools
Hot glue gun and glue sticks
Needles: hand-sewing

lengths. Refer to General Instructions for Twisted Rosebud on page 18. Fold each ribbon into a twisted rosebud.

6. Refer to General Instructions for Rose on page 16. Using peach wire-edge ribbon, make Double Rose Variation on page 16.

7. Glue rose, rosebuds, and leaves to front of cap as shown on Satin Cap Placement.

Satin Cap Placement

Scissors: fabric
Thread: coordinating

Instructions

1. Using peach organdy/satin striped sheer ribbon, make a Multi-Loop Bow on page 14 with 5" ribbon tails.

2. Refer to General Instructions for Fork Cut on page 12. Fork-cut ribbon ends using fabric scissors.

3. Using hot glue gun and glue stick, attach bow to center front of cap.

4. Cut sage wire-edge ribbon into six 6" lengths. Refer to General Instructions for Pulled Petal or Leaf on page 15. Make each ribbon into a pulled leaf.

5. Cut dk. peach wire-edge ribbon into two equal

Hat Stand

by Vanessa-Ann Designers
Materials
Willow branches: corkscrew (10-12)
Embroidery ribbon: 4mm olive green (1 yd.), yellow (2 yds.)
Wire-edge ribbon: ⅞"-wide olive green chiffon (1⅜ yds.), lavender chiffon (2 yds.); ⅞"-wide teal ombré taffeta (½ yd.); 1½"-wide lavender taffeta (⅜ yd.); 2¼"-wide

1. Crisscross willow branches together, leaving 8" legs.

2. Using florist wire and hot glue gun and glue stick, tightly wrap and glue branches. Let glue dry.

3. Wrap raffia around center of branches to cover florist wire. Tuck raffia into itself to secure.

4. Using fabric scissors, cut olive green chiffon wire-edge ribbon into eight 6" lengths. Refer to General Instructions for Pulled Petal or Leaf on page 15. Make each ribbon into a pulled leaf.

5. Using wire cutters, cut florist wire into four 3" lengths, two 5" lengths, one 4" length and one 6" length. Set 3" wires aside.

6. Attach three pulled leaves to each 5" wire and one leaf each to the 4" and 6" wires. Wrap wires with florist tape.

7. Cut 1½"-wide lavender wire-edge ribbon into four 4" lengths. Refer to General Instructions for Seed Pod on page 17. Make each ribbon into a seed pod.

lavender taffeta (1½ yds.); 2¼"-wide lavender chiffon (½ yd.)
Fabric: muslin (¼ yd.)
Double-sided fusible web (⅓ yd.)
Raffia
Dried berries
Leaves: paper (2 stems), velvet (2)
Stamen: beaded (5), small yellow (4)
Beads: medium pearl (2)

Florist wire: gauge
Florist tape: green
Cotton balls (5)
Paddle wire: 24-26 gauge
Stuffing

General Supplies & Tools
Hot glue gun and glue sticks
Needles: hand-sewing
Scissors: fabric
Sewing machine
Thread: coordinating
Wire cutters

8. Cut yellow embroidery ribbon into eighteen 4" lengths. Knot one end of each ribbon. Group ribbons into six clusters of three to form stamens for trumpets. Vary length of each ribbon in each cluster by cutting lengths between 1½"-2½".

9. Cut olive green embroidery ribbon into six 6" lengths. Thread needle. Knot one end of each ribbon. Thread three stamens onto one ribbon as shown in Diagram A.

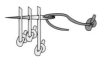

Diagram A

10. Cut 2¼"-wide lavender wire-edge ribbon into three 5" lengths. Cut lavender chiffon wire-edge ribbon into three 5" lengths. Refer to General Instructions for Trumpet on page 18. Make each ribbon into a trumpet, using stamen clusters from Steps 8 and 9 as centers.

11. Insert needle with stamen into trumpet. Pull stamens to top as shown in Diagram B. Take a
continued on page 59

Bird Pattern   Enlarge 220%

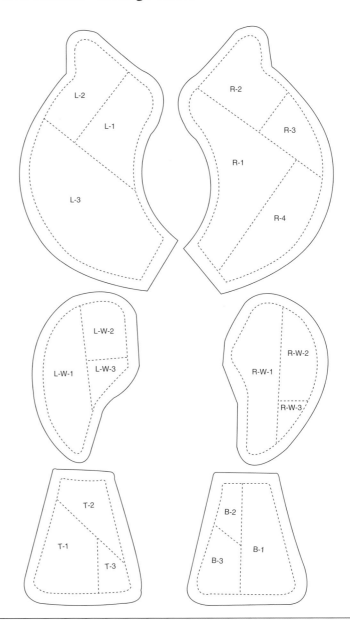

Chevron Stitch

Bring needle up at A, down at B, up at C, down at D, up at E, down at F, back up at G, down at H, up at I, and down at J.

Cretan Stitch

Working left to right come up at A and go down at B and up at C. Go down to the right at D and up at E. Continue working in this manner until area is filled.

continued from page 58

small stitch at top of trumpet flower to anchor stamens in flower. Repeat for each trumpet.

Diagram B

12. Cut ⅜"-wide lavender wire-edge ribbon into twenty 3½" lengths. Refer to General Instructions for Pulled Petal or Leaf on page 15. Make each ribbon into a pulled petal.

13. Evenly space five pulled petals around one small yellow stamen to form a flower. Secure base of petals to stamen with small amount of paddle wire. Attach flower to 3" florist wires. Wrap wires with green florist tape to cover.

14. Glue berries, beaded stamens, all leaves, ribbon flowers, and seed pods to raffia and branches as desired.

15. To make bird, enlarge Bird Pattern on page 58. Transfer design onto muslin fabric. Cut two each of wing patterns. Cut one each of tail and bird body patterns.

16. Using enlarged Bird Pattern and remaining 2¼"-wide lavender wire-edge ribbon, cut two each of R-W-1, R-W-2, L-W-1, and L-W-3. Cut one each of R-1, R-2, R-3, L-1, L-3, T-2, T-3, B-1, and B-3 pattern pieces. Allowing ¼" seam, stitch ribbon together as needed to match muslin pieces.

17. Use teal ombré wire-edge ribbon to cut two each of R-W-3 and L-W-2. Cut one each of R-4, L-2, T-1, and B-2 pattern pieces. Allowing ¼" seam, stitch ribbon together as needed to match muslin pieces.

18. Using fusible web and following manufacturer's instructions, fuse ribbon to muslin pieces.

19. Right sides together, sew top and bottom tail pieces, and top and bottom wing pieces together, leaving an opening at small end of tail and inner wings. Turn right side out. Hem-stitch openings closed.

20. Right sides together, sew left and right body pieces together, leaving an opening at back end of body to insert tail. Stitch opening closed. Tack wings to body.

21. Use Chevron and Cretan stitches on page 58 to embellish bird along seams as desired.

22. Sew pearl beads to both sides of bird's head.

23. Glue bird to hat stand in desired location.

Bird Placement

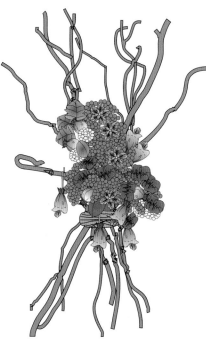

Hat Stand Placement

Spring Hat

2. Using hot glue gun and glue stick, attach a pearl stamen cluster to center of each rose.

3. Cut one length of dk. green wire-edge ribbon to fit as a hat band. With seam at center front, glue in place.

4. Using remaining dk. green wire-edge ribbon, cut two 4" lengths. Refer to General Instructions for Fork Cut on page 12. Fork-cut one end of each ribbon.

5. Cut remaining dk. green ribbon into two equal lengths. Loop each ribbon in half. Twist ends together to hold.

6. Glue fork-cut ribbon to each front side of hat. Glue ribbon loop to each front side of hat as shown in Diagram A.

Diagram A

7. Center and glue roses to front of hat. Glue velvet leaf

Materials
Straw hat
Wire-edge ribbon: 2¼"-wide pale yellow (3 yds.); 2¾"-wide dk. green (1½ yds.)
Leaves: velvet (2 clusters)
Stamen: pearl (3 clusters)

General Supplies & Tools
Hot glue gun and glue sticks

Scissors: fabric
Thread: coordinating

Instructions
1. Using fabric scissors, cut pale yellow wire-edge ribbon into three equal lengths. Refer to General Instructions for Rose on page 16. Make each ribbon into a rose, using Antique Rose Variation.

clusters between roses. Refer to Spring Hat Placement.

Spring Hat Placement

Materials

Vase: 4" x 6" oval

Wire-edge ribbon: ⅜"-wide dusty pink taffeta (6¼ yds.); ⅞"-wide pink ombré taffeta (1¾ yds.), purple ombré taffeta (4¼ yds.); 1½"-wide olive green taffeta ombré (7⅜ yds.)

Pom-poms: black, medium (17), small (7)

Glass pebbles: black

Floral styrofoam oasis

Florist tape: olive green

Stamens: black and white (24 clusters)

Stem wire: 16-18 gauge

General Supplies & Tools

Hot glue gun and glue sticks

Knife

Needles: hand-sewing

Scissors: fabric

Thread: coordinating

Wire cutters

Instructions

1. Using knife, trim and shape floral styrofoam oasis to fit vase. Using hot glue gun and glue stick, attach oasis to inside of vase.

2. Using fabric scissors, cut olive green ombré wire-edge ribbon into seventy-two 3 ½" lengths. Refer to General Instructions for Pointed Petal or Leaf on page 15. Make each ribbon into a pointed leaf, using No-Sew Variation on page 15.

3. Using wire cutters, cut stem wire into twenty-four 4" lengths, ten 12" lengths, and twenty-four 10" lengths.

4. Refer to General Instructions for Pointed Petal or Leaf on page 15. Using olive green florist tape and

4" wires, wrap leaves in clusters of three.

5. Cut dusty pink wire-edge ribbon into ninety 2½" lengths. Refer to General Instructions for Pointed Petal or Leaf on page 15. Make each ribbon into a pointed leaf, using No-Sew Variation on page 16.

6. Using florist tape and 12" wires, make ten 9-bud stems, using Cluster Variation on page 15.

7. Cut purple ombré wire-edge ribbon into seventeen 9" lengths. Refer to General Instructions for Bachelor Button on page 10. Make each ribbon into a bachelor button, stitching along dark purple edge of ten ribbons and along light purple edge of seven ribbons.

8. Cut pink ombré wire-edge taffeta ribbon into seven 9"-lengths. Make each ribbon into a bachelor button, stitching along light pink edge of three ribbons and along dark pink edge of four ribbons.

9. Gently open stamens with fingers. Glue a small pom-pom to center of each

pink flower and a medium pom-pom to center of each purple flower. Refer to Diagram A.

Diagram A

10. Wrap flowers and leaf clusters together with remaining pink ombré wire-edge ribbon as desired.

11. Arrange flowers and bud stems in vase as desired. Gently bend and shape wires as desired. Refer to Fantasy Flower Placement.

Fantasy Flower Placement

Heart Wreath

Materials
Twig wreath: heart-shaped
Wire-edge ribbon: ⅝"-wide olive green ombré taffeta (2¼ yds.); ⅞"-wide white/magenta ombré taffeta (2⅛ yds.); 1½"-wide white/magenta ombré taffeta (1⅞ yds.), dk. pink ombré taffeta (2¾ yds.)
Stamens: black and white (15 clusters), pearl (1 cluster), yellow (1)
Florist tape: dk. green
Leaves: velvet (11); maidenhair fern (1 stem)
Cotton balls: small (15)
Stem wire: 16-18 gauge

General Supplies & Tools
Hot glue gun and glue sticks
Needles: hand-sewing
Scissors: fabric
Thread: coordinating
Wire cutters

Instructions
1. Using fabric scissors, cut olive green ombré wire-edge ribbon into thirteen 6" lengths. Refer to General Instructions for Pulled Petal or Leaf on page 15. Make each ribbon into a pulled leaf, pulling wire on lightest edge of ribbon.

edge of ribbon. Using hot glue gun and glue stick, place a small line of glue down the center seam of each petal. Glue seam closed to finish each petal.

5. Using wire cutters, cut florist wire into one 4" length and three 15" lengths.

6. Using hot glue gun and glue stick, attach yellow stamen bead to center of pearl cluster stamen. Attach stamen to 4" wire.

7. Using stem wire, attach white/magenta pulled petals to pearl/bead stamen to form a flower. Attach base of petals to stamen stem with stem wire. Begin with smallest petals at center and work randomly with medium and large petals until all are used. Refer to Diagram A.

Diagram A

2. Cut dk. pink ombré wire-edge ribbon into two 12" lengths and two 18" lengths. Refer to General Instructions for Rose on page 16. With darkest edge of ribbon on outside, make each ribbon into a rose.

3. Cut remaining dk. pink ombré ribbon into five 8" lengths. Refer to General Instructions for Twisted Rosebud on page 18. Make each ribbon into a twisted rosebud.

4. Cut ⅞"-wide white/magenta wire-edge ribbon into two 6" lengths, four 8" lengths, and three 10" lengths. Refer to General Instructions for Pulled Petal or Leaf on page 15. Make each ribbon into a pulled petal, pulling wire on darkest

8. Cut 1½"-wide white/magenta wire-edge ribbon into fifteen 4½" lengths. Refer to General Instructions for Bleeding Heart on page 10. Make each ribbon into a bleeding heart with darkest edge of ribbon at top of flower.

9. Cut fifteen 3" pieces of wire. Using glue, attach one piece of wire at top of each bleeding heart. Cut three 12" pieces of stem wire. Attach four bleeding hearts and five pulled leaves. Attach five bleeding hearts and five leaves to second wire. Attach six bleeding hearts and four leaves to third wire. Bend and shape wires to fit wreath.

10. Arrange and glue flowers and leaves to wreath as shown on Heart Wreath Placement. Fill in with maidenhair fern and velvet leaves as desired.

Heart Wreath Placement

Single Rose Pillow

Materials
Fabric: taffeta, crinkled-pleated burgundy 10"-square (2);
cherub print, scrap
Wire-edge ribbon: 1½"-wide olive green taffeta (½ yd.); 2¾"-wide dk. iridescent burgundy taffeta (1 yd.)

Button kit with fabric-covered cherub
Pillow form: 9"
Thread: burgundy

General Supplies & Tools
Hot glue gun and glue sticks
Needles: hand-sewing
Sewing machine
Scissors: fabric

Instructions
1. With right sides together,

sew ¼" seam on all three sides of 10" squares of burgundy taffeta. Turn fabric square inside out and fill with pillow form. Stitch opened side closed.

2. Using fabric scissors, cut olive green wire-edge ribbon into two 9" lengths. Refer to General Instructions for Pulled Petal or Leaf on page 15. Make each ribbon into a pulled leaf.

3. Refer to General Instructions for Rose on page 16. Using dk. iridescent burgundy wire-edge ribbon, make a rose.

4. Make fabric button following manufacturer's instructions. Center cherub on button.

5. Using hot glue gun and glue stick, attach cherub button to center of rose. Glue leaves underneath rose.

6. Glue rose arrangement to center top of pillow as shown on Single Rose Pillow Placement.

Single Rose Pillow Placement

Hat Box

Materials
Hat box: burgundy fabric-covered octagonal
Wire-edge ribbon: 1½"-wide burgundy taffeta (2 yds.), dk. iridescent burgundy taffeta (1 yd.); 2¾"-wide dk. iridescent burgundy taffeta (2½ yds.)

General Supplies & Tools
Hot glue gun and glue sticks
Needles: hand-sewing
Scissors: fabric
Thread: coordinating

Instructions
1. Using fabric scissors, cut burgundy wire-edge ribbon into nine 8" lengths. Refer to

General Instructions for Twisted Rosebud on page 18. Make each ribbon into a twisted rosebud.

2. Refer to General Instructions for Stitched Flower on page 17. Make each like-size interval into a stitched flower. Using 2¾"-wide dk. burgundy wire-edge ribbon, mark three 5" lengths, four 7" lengths, and five 9" lengths on ribbon.

Gather three 5" intervals, Row 1, into a circle. Stitch petals to hold together. Gather four 7" intervals, Row 2, into a circle. Surround Row 1. Stitch petals to hold together. Gather five 9" intervals, Row 3, into a circle. Surround Row 2. Stitch petals to hold together to complete Rows 1-3 of stitched flower.

3. Glue one twisted rosebud to center of stitched flower.

4. Glue stitched flower to top center of box lid as shown in Diagram A.

Diagram A

5. Gently swag 1½"-wide dk. burgundy wire-edge ribbon around side of box lid, twisting ribbon at beginning and ending of each swag to hold. Secure with hot glue at center of each panel, and make certain ribbon ends swag together. Glue a rosebud at each twist. Conceal beginning and ending of ribbon under a rosebud.

Hat Box Placement

Lily Wreath

Materials
Wreath: grapevine 16"
Wire-edge ribbon: 1½"-wide white taffeta (3 yds.), orange ombré taffeta (4½ yds.), yellow ombré taffeta (3⅛ yds.), green ombré taffeta (¾ yd.); ⅞"-wide orange ombré, taffeta (⅝ yd.), green ombré taffeta (4 yds.)
Satin ribbon: ¼"- wide, yellow

(7½ yds.)
Branches: premade, ivy
Chenille stems: yellow (10), brown (1)
Florist tape: green, pale green, brown
Paddle wire: 24-26 gauge
Stamens: red, white
Stem wire: 16-18 gauge

General Supplies & Tools
Hot glue gun and glue sticks
Needles: hand-sewing
Pliers: needlenose
Thread: coordinating
Marking pen: brown, indelible

Instructions
1. Cut 1½"orange ombré wire-edge ribbon into eighteen 9" lengths. Refer to General Instructions for Boat Leaf on page 10. Make each ribbon into a petal using boat leaf technique.

2. Using marking pen, dot each petal with dots to simulate tiger lily petals.

3. Cut brown chenille stem into three 3" pieces. Using needlenose pliers, roll over one end into a ball.

4. Cut yellow chenille stems into eighteen 3" pieces. Fold one end of stem into a "T" shape. Using pale green florist tape, wrap bottom of "T" to cover yellow.

5. Cut ⅞" green ombré wire-edge ribbon into eleven 12" lengths. Refer to General Instructions for Boat Leaf on page 10. Make each ribbon into a boat leaf.

6. Refer to General Instructions for Lily on page 14. Make orange petals into a lily, using items from Steps 1-5.

7. Cut wire-edge white ribbon into five 21" lengths. Refer to General Instructions for Stitched Flower on page 17, marking each length into six 3½" intervals.

8. Cut ⅞" orange ombré wire-edge ribbon into five 4" pieces. Refer to General Instructions for Trumpet on page 18. Make each ribbon into a trumpet. Attach red and white stamens to a 9" stem wire. Insert stamen in center of orange trumpet.

Secure stamens in trumpet with a small amount of glue.

9. Refer to General Instructions for Narcissus on page 14. Make five narcissuses, using remaining items from Step 5, and items from Step 7, and 8.

10. Cut stem wire into three 18-20" lengths. Cover each wire with brown florist tape. Cut yellow satin into 2" lengths. Refer to General Instructions for Forsythia on page 12. Attach 19-25 forsythias to each stem using brown stem wire. Stagger pattern of placement. Use all forsythias.

11. Refer to General Instructions for Multi-Loop Bow on page 14. Using yellow ombré ribbon, make a multi-loop bow with eight 9" loops. One tail should be 18", the remaining tail should be approximately 22".

12. Secure loops with small amount of wire to hold.

13. Glue bow to wreath.

14. Arrange flowers as shown on Lily Wreath Placement. Arrange forsythia branches as shown. Trim stems as needed. Glue stems in place. Add lilies and narcissus to arrangement. Fill in with ivy as desired.

15. Arrange bow tails throughout flowers. Glue in place to hold.

Lily Wreath Placement

Blossom Vase

Materials
Vase
Wire-edge ribbon: 1½"-wide, yellow ombré taffeta; ⅜"-wide white taffeta (4⅞ yds.); ⅞"-wide green ombré taffeta (4½ yds.)
Chenille stems: yellow (5), brown (1)
Florist tape: brown, green, pale green
Moss
Oasis
Stamens: pearl (9), yellow (9)
Stem wire: 16-18 gauge
Wire cutters

General Tools & Supplies

Needles: hand-sewing
Pliers: needlenose
Scissors: fabric
Thread: coordinating

Instructions

1. Using wire cutters, cut two 12" pieces and fifteen 2" pieces of stem wire for two apple blossom branches. Wrap each piece of stem wire with brown florist tape.

2. Cut wire-edge yellow ombré ribbon into eighteen 9" lengths. Refer to General Instructions for Boat Leaf on page 10. Make each ribbon into a petal using boat leaf technique, stitching along darkest edge of ribbon. Set aside. Cut wire-edged green ombré ribbon into six 12" lengths. Make each ribbon into a boat leaf. Set aside.

3. Cut brown chenille stem into three 3" pieces. Using needlenose pliers roll one end into a ball. Cut yellow chenille stems into eighteen 3" pieces. Fold one end of each piece into a "T" shape. Using pale green florist tape, wrap bottom of "T" to cover yellow.

4. Refer to General Instructions for Lily on page 14. Make three lily flowers using yellow petals.

5. Cut wire-edge white ribbon into fifty 3½" lengths. Refer to General Instructions for Pulled Petal or Leaf on page 15. Make each ribbon into a pulled petal. Set aside.

6. Cut wire-edge green ombré ribbon into fifteen 6" lengths. Refer to General Instructions for Pulled Petal or Leaf on page 15. Make each ribbon into a pulled leaf. Set aside.

7. Glue pearl stamens around yellow stamen for a total of nine stamens. Attach stamens to stem wire.

8. Refer to General Instructions for Apple Blossom on page 9. Make nine apple blossoms. Make five apple blossom buds by attaching each remaining white pulled petal to 2" stem wire cut in Step 1. Wrap stem wire with green florist tape to secure apple blossom and apple blossom bud.

9. Refer for Blossom Vase Placement to assemble two apple blossom branches. For one: (one 12" and seven 2" pieces stem wire, four apple blossoms, three apple blossom buds, eight pulled leaves.) Attach a total of eight pulled leaves to branch one. Secure pulled petals with brown florist tape. For branch two: (one 12" and seven 2" pieces stem wire, five apple blossoms, two apple blossom buds, seven pulled petals. Repeat for remaining apple blossom branch.

10. Insert oasis into vase. Secure with craft glue. Cover oasis with moss. Insert lilies and apple blossoms into oasis. Arrange as shown on Blossom Vase Placement.

**Blossom Vase
Placement**

Katheryn Tidwell Foutz

Katheryn Tidwell Foutz has always delighted in the creative process. She was raised in a very loving and supportive family who encouraged her creative endeavors, which, more often than not, ended up in disaster!

Katheryn enjoys designing, writing, and teaching many types of crafts from sewing and needlework to wood-working, clay and fabric sculpting, floral design, and doll making. Her love of ribbons and Victorian ribbon work reflect through all of these mediums. She also regularly teaches crafting on "Aleene's Creative Living" television program.

Katheryn believes that in design, as in life, you should try to turn your stumbling blocks into stepping stones. She says that you should never fret over making a mistake, but that you should find joy in the fact that you've created a new variation.

Artist's photo courtesy of Aleene's Creative Living Magazine Director of photography Craig Cook. Designer/Stylist Carolyn Bainbridge.

ribbons. Lay ribbons side by side and machine-zigzag together to create amulet fabric.

2. Fold one end of fabric down ¼" twice. Using a hand-sewing needle and co-ordinating thread, hand-stitch to hem.

3. Measure and mark ½" from opposite end of fabric. With right sides together, fold fabric in half length-wise. Machine-stitch across width of fabric at mark. Open fabric so right sides are facing out and press flat to form pointed top flap.

4. Refer to General Instructions for Transferring on page 9. Enlarge Inspiring Amulet Transfer Pattern on page 71. Center and transfer design onto fabric.

5. Using embroidery and chenille needles, embroider fabric following Inspiring Amulet Stitch Guide on page 71.

6. When embroidery is completed, use number 10 sharp needle and thread to

Note: Please refer to a book on basic embroidery stitches to complete this project.

Materials
Brocade ribbon: 1½"-wide ivory (⅜ yd.)
Embroidery ribbon: 4mm lt. green (½ yd.), med. green (½ yd.), ivory (½ yd.), lt. rose (¾ yd.), med. rose (½ yd.)
Jacquard ribbon: ¾"-wide tan with pink florals (⅜ yd.)
Brass charms: bee, heart
Cording: ⅛"-wide ivory (1 yd.)
Floss: metallic gold

General Supplies & Tools
Fabric marker: air soluble
Index card: 3" x 5"
Iron/ironing board
Needles: chenille, size 22; embroidery; hand-sewing
Scissors: fabric
Sewing machine
Thread: coordinating

Instructions
1. Using fabric scissors, cut a 9½" length from both brocade and jacquard

tack all ribbon ends to back of ribbon.

7. Measure and mark 3¼" from hemmed edge. With wrong sides together, fold fabric in half lengthwise. Machine-stitch across width of fabric at mark. Open so right sides are facing out and press fabric flat to form point for bottom of amulet.

8. Place fabric front side down on soft, white cloth and press with iron.

9. Cut one 10" length from med. rose embroidery ribbon. Tie ribbon into a 1½"-wide bow. Using a hand-sewing needle and co-ordinating thread, tack ribbon in place. Tack heart charm to knot of bow. Tack bee charm to flap. Refer to Inspiring Amulet Placement.

10. Fold fabric to form purse. Hand-stitch sides together and fold flap down.

11. Mark center of cording and place cording at bottom of purse. Using lt. green embroidery ribbon, whip-stitch cording to purse. Knot ends of cording.

12. Wrap lt. rose, ivory, and metallic gold floss length-wise around index card six times. Slip a strand of floss under one end of wraps and tie into knot for top of tassel. Slip wraps off of index card and tie floss around wraps ½" from top of tassel. Cut bottom of wraps. Tack tassel to tip of purse as shown in Inspiring Amulet Placement.

Inspiring Amulet Stitch Guide

Description	Ribbon	Stitch
1. Rosebud Center	med. rose	Ribbon Stitch
2. Rosebud Petal	lt. rose	Ribbon Stitch
3. Leaf	med. green	Ribbon Stitch
4. Rosebud Base	med. green	French Knot
5. Rosebud Stem	med. green	Rolled Straight Stitch
6. Leaf	med. green	Ribbon Stitch
7. Leaf	lt. green	Ribbon Stitch
8. "I"	metallic gold floss	Chain Stitch
9. Letters	metallic gold floss	Stem Stitch
10. Flap Decor	metallic gold floss	Herringbone Stitch
11. Purse Decor	metallic gold floss	Straight Stitch

Inspiring Amulet Transfer Pattern Enlarge 200%

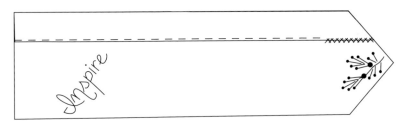

Inspiring Amulet Stitch Guide

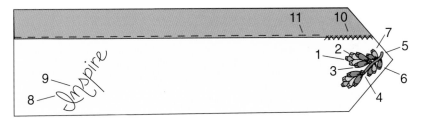

Inspiring Amulet Placement

Sisterhood Pillow

General Supplies & Tools

Hot glue gun and glue sticks
Iron/ironing board
Marker: permanent black
Needle: hand-sewing
Scissors: fabric
Sewing machine
Thread: coordinating

Instructions

1. Using fabric scissors, cut lt. green moiré taffeta fabric into two 5" squares. Cut two 4½" squares from quilt batting. Refer to General Instructions for Baste Stitch on page 9. Using a hand-sewing needle and coordinating thread, baste quilt batting to fabric. Fold edges under ½" and press to form pillow front and pillow back.

2. Measure and mark green/gold wired silk fabric at a 5" and 10" interval. Clip marks and tear fabric into two strips. Hand-stitch ends together to form one large strip.

3. Sew a gather-stitch along one long edge of strip. Gather strip into a ruffle to

Materials

Fabric: lt. green moiré taffeta (¼ yd.); green/gold wired silk (⅜ yd.)
Sheer ribbon: ⅞"-wide green with gold edging (⅓ yd.)
Wire-edge ribbon: ⅜"-wide gold mesh (2 yds.); ½"-wide white/gold net (¼ yd.); ⅝"-wide peach (⅝ yd.); 1½"-wide sheer cream with gold edging (¼ yd.)

Beads: white seed
Butterfly: blue net, small
Floral stamens: white
Tatted lace: scraps
Leaves: silk (1); velvet (3)
Quilt batting
Ribbon roses: peach swirl, miniature (3)
Stuffing
Veiling: 8"-wide green hat (¼ yd.)

fit around pillow front and hand-stitch in place.

4. Lay pillow front on pillow back and hand-stitch together, leaving one side open for stuffing. Stuff pillow and hand-stitch opening closed. Machine-stitch ruffle seams together.

5. Tack tatted lace to upper left corner of pillow front. Randomly sew white seed beads to lace. Refer to Sisterhood Pillow Placement.

6. Refer to General Instructions for Rose on page 16. Make peach wire-edge ribbon into a rose.

7. Fold green sheer ribbon with gold edging into two pairs of 1" loops. Tack loops together at base of loops to form a plume.

8. Cut sheer cream with gold edging wire-edge ribbon into two equal lengths. Refer to General Instructions for Single Petal on page 17. Make each ribbon into a single petal.

9. Refer to Sisterhood Pillow Placement. Using a glue gun and glue sticks, attach velvet leaves over

tatted lace. Hot-glue rose on top of leaves. Hot-glue green sheer ribbon plume under rose, and hot-glue sheer cream ribbon petals under velvet leaves. Hot-glue stamen between ribbon loops. Hot-glue butterfly to edge of rose.

10. Tack green hat veiling across upper right corner of pillow front.

11. Gently pull to widen white/gold net ribbon. Pinch ribbon together at 1" intervals. Tack ribbon across

bottom edge of pillow front. Randomly sew white seed beads to peach swirl roses. Evenly space roses on ribbon and hot-glue in place.

12. Cut gold net wire-edge ribbon into four equal lengths. Tie each ribbon into a bow with 4" tails. Tack each bow to corner of pillow.

13. Using a black permanent marker, write desired word or message on silk leaf. Hot-glue silk leaf under velvet leaf.

Sisterhood Pillow Placement

73

Miracle Pillow

General Supplies & Tools

Embroidery hoop
Fabric marker: air-soluble
Hot glue gun and glue sticks
Iron/ironing board
Needles: embroidery; hand-
    sewing
Scissors: fabric
Straight pins
Thread: coordinating

Instructions

1. Enlarge Pattern A on page 75. Refer to General Instructions for Transferring on page 9. Transfer verse to center of ivory taffeta fabric. Place fabric in embroidery hoop.

2. Using an embroidery needle and metallic gold embroidery floss, embroider verse onto fabric.

3. Center and pin enlarged Pattern A over embroidered taffeta fabric. Using fabric scissors, cut out heart ½" larger than guide-line. Clip curves. Turn edge under and press. Using a hand-sewing needle and thread, tack heart to pillow front center.

Note: Please refer to a book on basic embroidery stitches to complete this project.

Materials

Pillow: purchased, 16" square, ivory brocade
Fabric: ivory taffeta (⅓ yd.)
Embroidery ribbon: 4mm ivory (1 yd.)
Sheer ribbon: 2"-wide ivory with satin edges and gold filaments (⅓ yd.)
Wire-edge ribbon: ⅞"-wide gold mesh (1 yd.), lt. gold mesh (½ yd.); 1½"-wide gold mesh (⅓ yd.), lt. gold mesh (1½ yds.), white taffeta with gold edges (¾ yd.); 2¼"-wide white taffeta with gold edges (1 yd.), ivory/gold brocade with gold edges (½ yd.)
Doily: 6" square ecru lace
Embroidery floss: metallic gold; ivory
Lace: 2"-wide ivory (¼ yd.)

Expect
a
Miracle

to top right corner of heart. Refer to Miracle Pillow Placement on page 76.

9. Sew a gather stitch along bottom edge of lace. Pull gather and shape lace into a fan. Hot-glue lace fan under top right outside edge of flower.

10. Cut four 4" lengths from ⅞"-wide lt. gold mesh wire-edge ribbon. Cut remaining 1½"-wide lt. gold mesh wire-edge ribbon into three equal lengths. Cut 1½"-wide gold mesh wire-edge ribbon into two equal lengths. Refer to General Instructions for Folded Leaf on page 12. Make each ribbon into a folded leaf.

11. Hot-glue leaves as shown in Miracle Pillow Placement on opposite page.

12. Tack doily to pillow front, above upper left corner of heart.

4. Using an embroidery needle and ivory embroidery floss, sew a running stitch onto pillow front, around edge of heart.

5. Twist and weave ivory embroidery ribbon through running stitch. Weave two strands of metallic gold embroidery floss through running stitch.

6. Cut five 7" lengths from gold mesh wire-edge ribbon. Tie a knot in center of each ribbon. Lay ribbons side-by-side with knots at top. Sew a gather stitch ½" above the bottom edges. Pull gather to form a cluster for center of flower. Set aside.

7. Divide 1½"-wide white taffeta with gold edges wire-edge ribbon into five equal intervals. Divide 2¼"-wide white taffeta with gold edges wire-edge ribbon into six equal intervals. Divide 1½"-wide lt. gold mesh wire-edge ribbon into three equal intervals. Divide sheer ivory with satin edges and gold filament ribbon into three equal intervals. Divide ivory/gold brocade with gold edges ribbon into three equal intervals. Refer to General Instructions for Multiple-Petal Section on page 14. Make each ribbon into a multiple-petal section.

8. Layer and tack petals around cluster as in Diagram A. Using a hot glue gun and glue sticks, hot-glue flower

Miracle Pillow Placement

Materials

Hand mirror: 12"

Fabric: ivory taffeta (¼ yd.)

Grosgrain ribbon: ⅜"-wide antique white (1 yd.)

Satin ribbon: ¼"-wide ivory (1 yd.); ⅝"-wide lt. peach (1 yd.)

Sheer ribbon: ⅝"-wide ivory stripe (1 yd.), white with gold edging (⅓ yd.); ⅞"-wide cream (½ yd.); 1½"-wide cream (⅓ yd.)

Wire-edge ribbon: ⅝"-wide lt. peach (3¼ yds.), cream (⅓ yd.); 1¼"-wide gold net (¼ yd.)

Ribbon roses: ivory swirl, miniature (3)

Brass charms: bee; leaf stems (3); ¾" letters B, E (3), I, L, V; rose

Cording: ⅛"-wide metallic gold (⅝ yd.)

Fusible web (¼ yd.)

Gimp: ivory (⅞ yd.)

Lace: 3" x 6" ivory, flat crocheted; medallions (2)

Quilt batting: lightweight (¼ yd.)

General Supplies & Tools

Foam core board: 12" square

Glue: craft; industrial-strength

Iron/ironing board

Needle: hand-sewing
Fabric marker: air-soluble
Scissors: fabric
Straight pins
Thread: coordinating

Instructions

1. Using fabric scissors, cut an 8" square from fusible web. Lay fusible web face up on foam core board. Refer to General Instructions for Ribbon Weaving on pages 15-16. Weave and pin the grosgrain, satin, and ⅜"-wide ivory stripe sheer ribbons until the fusible web is covered. Following manu-facturer's instructions, fuse ribbons.

2. Diagonally lay mirror over woven ribbons. Using a disappearing marking pen, trace around mirror and cut out.

3. Lay mirror on taffeta fabric. Trace around mirror and handle and cut out. Repeat process on quilt batting.

4. Fuse woven ribbons to right side of taffeta fabric.

5. Trace around handle only on taffeta fabric and quilt batting and cut out.

6. Apply a thin layer of craft glue to back of mirror and handle. Glue quilt batting in place. Apply glue to top of batting and attach woven ribbon/taffeta fabric to batting. Turn mirror over and repeat process for handle only, using batting and taffeta fabric.

7. Using ⅞"-wide cream sheer ribbon, wrap handle, tucking and gluing ends under.

8. Cut flat crocheted lace to fit diagonally across top of mirror back as shown in Diagram A. Glue lace edges to woven ribbons.

Diagram A

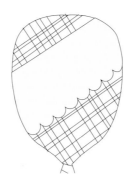

9. Glue gimp around outside edge of mirror and handle. Glue metallic gold cording around top edge of mirror back.

10. Cut one 10" length from cream wire-edge ribbon. Refer to General Instructions for Ruching on page 16.

Using a hand-sewing needle and coordinating thread, ruch ribbon and pull threads until ribbon measures 5". Glue ribbon on top edge of lace.

11. Cut two 9" lengths from lt. peach wire-edge ribbon. Refer to General Instructions for Multiple-Petal Section on page 14. Make each ribbon into a five-petal section. Clip leaves from swirl ribbon roses and glue one in center of each five-petal section. Glue one flower to top of mirror back. Glue remaining swirl ribbon rose to left of flower. Using industrial-strength glue, attach brass leaf stem charms to sides of flower.

12. Glue the B-E-L-I-E-V-E letters, bee, rose, and leaf stem in place as shown in Diagram B.

Diagram B

13. Using craft glue, attach lace medallions to top front and back of handle.

14. Tie 1½"-wide cream sheer ribbon into a bow. Glue bow to top handle, on back of mirror over lace medallion.

15. Cut gold net ribbon into two equal lengths. Refer to General Instructions for Folded Leaf on page 12. Make each ribbon into a folded leaf. Glue leaves to top of white sheer ribbon bow. Glue remaining five-petal section over folded leaves.

16. Pull wires on both sides of remaining lt. peach wire-edge ribbon. Gather ribbon to fit around front edge of mirror and glue in place.

17. Refer to General Instructions for Rose on page 16. Make cream wire-edge ribbon into a rose. Glue rose to top of lace medallion on handle front.

18. Tie white with gold edging sheer ribbon into a bow. Glue bow beneath rose.

Floral Mirror Back & Front Placement

Materials
Pewter frame: 8" x 10"
Photo mat: 5" x 7" precut green rectangle
Picot-edge ribbon: ⅝"-wide ivory striped (½ yd.)
Sheer ribbon: 2"-wide rose with satin edges and gold filaments (½ yd.)
Wire-edge ribbon: ⅞"-wide rose (1 yd.), sage green (1¾ yds.); 1½"-wide frosty forest green (½ yd.); 1¾"-wide green sculptor (⅜ yd.)
Lace: 3"-wide cream antique (¼ yd.)
Trim: 2"-wide gold metallic fringe (¼ yd.)

General Supplies & Tools
Hot glue gun and glue sticks
Needle: hand-sewing
Thread: coordinating hand-quilting
Scissors: fabric

Instructions
1. Using fabric scissors, cut one 18" length from frosty forest green wire-edge ribbon. Fold ribbon into ½" pleats, folding the raw edges at either end under twice. Using a hand-sewing needle and coordinating thread, sew a gather stitch along the sides and bottom of the

pleated ribbon. Gently pull gather up to create a fan. Set aside. Repeat process on gold metallic fringe trim and cream antique lace.

2. Cut one 16" length from rose sheer ribbon. Refer to General Instructions for Folded & Rolled Rose on page 12. Make into folded and rolled rose.

3. Cut two 5" lengths from green sculptor wire-edge ribbon, and cut seven 3" lengths from sage green wire-edge ribbon. Refer to General Instructions for Folded Leaf on page 12. Make each ribbon into a folded leaf.

4. Twist remaining sage green wire-edge ribbon into a vine.

5. Cut three 12" lengths from rose wire-edge ribbon. Refer to General Instructions for Rose on page 16. Make each ribbon into a rose.

6. Layer gathered lace, pleated ribbon, and gold metallic fringe fans one atop the other as shown in Diagram A. Using a hot glue gun and glue sticks, attach fans to top of frame.

Diagram A

7. Hand-stitch folded and rolled rose to top of large folded leaves and tack in place. Glue rose to fans.

8. Arrange and glue vine, no-sew ribbon roses and small folded leaves on right side of frame as shown in Rose Frame Placement.

9. Embellish the green

precut mat by gluing strips of picot-edge ribbon to front of mat as shown. Place mat inside frame.

Frame of Roses Placement

Materials

Fabric: lt. green taffeta
  (¼ yd.); sheer gold wired
  silk (¼ yd.); vintage lace
  (¼ yd.)
Wire-edge ribbon: ½"-wide
  white/gold net (¼ yd.); ⅞"-
  wide purple/white ombré
  (1⅞ yds.); 1½"-wide lt. blue
  sheer (⅓ yd.); 3⅛"-wide
  gold net (1¼ yds.)
Buckram: ⅛ yd.
Floral stamens: white

Leaves: silk (2); velvet leaf
  branch; velvet (3)
Trim: ⅜"-wide gold/black
  fringe (¾ yd.)

General Supplies & Tools

Hot glue gun and glue sticks
Marker: black permanent
Needle: hand-sewing
Scissors: fabric
Sewing machine
Thread: coordinating

Instructions

1. Using fabric scissors, cut
two 6" x 9½" rectangles for
pillow front and back from
lt. green taffeta fabric. Lay
sheer gold wired silk fabric
over pillow front. Refer to
General Instructions for
Baste Stitch on page 9.
Using a hand-sewing needle
and coordinating thread,
baste wired silk fabric to
pillow front.

2. Cut a piece of vintage
lace fabric as desired
according to pattern in
fabric. Lay fabric across left
side of pillow front and
hand-stitch in place.

3. Gently pull to widen
white/gold net wire-edge
ribbon. Pinch ribbon
together at 1" intervals. Cut
one 4½" length from gold/
black fringe trim. Diagonally
lay ribbon and gold/black
fringe trim across right
corner of pillow front and
tack in place.

4. With right sides together
and a ⅝" seam, machine-
stitch pillow front to pillow
back, leaving an opening for

turning. Turn pillow right side out and stuff. Hand-stitch opening closed.

5. Hand-stitch gold net wire-edge ribbon around pillow edge, gathering ribbon at corners, for ruffle. Pinch ribbon together and tack to pillow edge at desired locations.

6. Cut two 3" squares and one 2" square from buckram. Cut purple/white ombré wire edge ribbon into three equal lengths. Refer to General Instructions for Buckram Rose on page 10. Using buckram squares, make each ribbon into a buckram rose.

7. Cut lt. blue sheer wire-edge ribbon into three equal lengths. Refer to General Instructions for Folded Leaf on page 12. Make each ribbon into a folded leaf. Shape leaves as desired.

8. Fold remaining gold/black fringe trim into three loops and tack ends together to form a plume.

9. Arrange roses, ribbon leaves, velvet leaves and leaf stem, plume, and stamens on pillow front and hot-glue in place. Refer to Romance & Love Pillow Placement.

10. Using a black permanent marker, write desired word or message on each silk leaf. Hot-glue leaves to pillow front.

Romance & Love Pillow Placement

Materials

Pillow: purchased, 16" square ivory tapestry with fringe

Sheer ribbon: ⅜"-wide white (¾ yd.); 1½"-wide pink with gold edging (1¼ yds.)

Wire-edge ribbon: ⅞"-wide lt. gold mesh; 1½"-wide striped gold mesh (1 yd.), sheer white with gold edging (1 yd.); 2"-wide white/gold net (1 yd.)

Beads: strung pearls (5 strands)

Bridal netting: 7"-wide white (1 yd.)

Buttons: jeweled heart, pearl teardrop, round antique silver, round glass, jeweled rectangle

Doily: 2" round taupe (2)

Fabric: flesh cotton (¼ yd.)

General Supplies & Tools

Acrylic paints: black, blue, dk. rose, white

Cosmetic blush: rose

Fabric marker: air soluble

Hot glue gun and glue sticks

Iron/ironing board

Needle: hand-sewing

Paintbrush: fine point

Pens, pigment : black, gold, dk. brown

Scissors: fabric

Sewing machine

Thread: coordinating

hand-sewing needle and coordinating thread, sew head to neck at chin, and neck to bodice. Place sewn pieces on pillow front and hand-stitch around outside edge to secure.

5. Cut striped gold mesh wire-edge ribbon and lt. gold mesh wire-edge ribbon into appropriate lengths for hair. Shape ribbons into wavy hair to cascade onto shoulders. Tack in place as shown on Dream Pillow Placement on opposite page.

6. Pinch and shape white/gold net wire-edge ribbon to cover bodice.

7. Cut one 9" length from sheer white with gold edging wire-edge ribbon. Shape into waves. Using a glue gun and glue sticks, hot-glue ribbon to bodice at tip of neck. Hot-glue jeweled heart button onto ribbon at tip of neck.

8. Tie sheer white ribbon into a 4" bow with cascading tails. Hot-glue bow below heart button. Hot-glue pearl teardrop button under knot of bow.

9. Cut bridal netting into one 24" length. Drape bridal netting below bodice and tack in place.

Instructions

1. Enlarge Dream Pillow Transfer Pattern below. Refer to General Instructions for Transferring on page 9. Transfer head and facial features, neck, and bodice patterns to flesh fabric.

Dream Pillow Transfer Pattern   Enlarge 400%

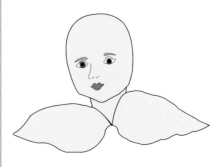

2. Using a dk. brown pen, trace over facial features. Using a fine point paint-brush, paint irises blue, pupils black, and lips dk. rose. Highlight pupil with a small white stroke. Lightly brush blush onto cheek area.

3. Machine-stitch around outline of head, neck, and bodice. Using fabric scissors, cut out patterns, leaving a ½" seam. Clip curves, turn under, and press.

4. Place head on neck, and neck on bodice. Using a

10. Cascade strung pearl beads down left side of hair. Hot-glue jeweled rectangle button to hair.

11. Tie pink with gold edging sheer ribbon into an 8" bow. Hot-glue bow in upper left corner of pillow. Knot ribbon tails 4" above ends. Cascade ribbon tails down side and across top of pillow front, tacking in place as desired. Refer to General Instructions for Fork Cut on page 12. Fork-cut ribbon ends.

12. Refer to General Instructions for Doily Flower on page 11. Make taupe doilies into a flower.

13. Hot-glue doily flower, round glass button, and round antique silver button to knot of bow as shown on Dream Pillow Placement.

14. Drape remaining bridal netting across upper left corner of pillow front, above bow. Tack in place.

15. Using black pen, center and write "Sweet Dreams" on remaining piece of sheer white with gold edging wire-edge ribbon. Outline words with gold pen. Shape ribbon into a banner. Tack ribbon to pillow front. Refer to General Instructions for Fork Cut on page 12. Cut ribbon ends.

Dream Pillow Placement

Lamp Shade Placement on page 84.

Lamp Shade

Materials
Lace lamp shade kit
Ribbon roses: premade, ivory swirl (12); ivory rosebuds, small (18)
Beads: strung pearl (1 yd.)
Brass charms: ¾" letters I, N, S, P, I, R, E

General Supplies & Tools
Hot glue gun and glue sticks
Needle: beading
Scissors: fabric
Straight pins
Thread: coordinating

Instructions
1. Apply lace to lamp shade according to kit instructions.

2. Using fabric scissors, trim lace away from alternating panels on lamp shade.

3. Using a hot glue gun and glue sticks, attach swirl roses around top edge of lamp shade as shown on Lamp Shade Placement on page 84.

4. Cut leaves from rosebuds. Glue three rosebuds in a cluster below every fourth swirl rose.

5. Glue rosebuds onto lace on shade panels.

Materials

Fabric: taupe brocade (⅓ yd.); brown silk (⅓ yd.)

Photo mat: 8½" x 10" precut oval

Cardboard, heavy: 9" x 11" rectangles (2)

Wire-edge ribbon, brown ombré: ⅞"-wide (3 yds.); 1½"-wide (3 yds.)

Cording: ⅛"-wide taupe (1 yd.)

Gimp: ½"-wide brown (1¾ yds.)

Poster board: ¼" x 6" strips (2); ¼" x 4" strip

Trim: ¼"-wide brown decorative (⅝ yd.)

General Supplies & Tools

Craft knife

Glue: craft; spray adhesive

Hot glue gun and glue sticks

Needle: hand-sewing

Pencil

Scissors: fabric

Thread: coordinating

Instructions

1. Using fabric scissors, cut seven 4" lengths from ⅞"-wide brown ombré wire-edge ribbon. Cut five 6" lengths from 1½"-wide brown ombré wire-edge ribbon. Refer to General Instructions for Folded Leaf on page 12.

6. Evenly drape pearls around lamp shade. Secure to lamp shade by hot-gluing pearls under swirl roses as shown.

7. Using straight pins, arrange and pin letters in place. Using a beading needle and coordinating thread, hand-stitch letters to lamp shade. Remove pins.

Lamp Shade Placement

Using a hand-sewing needle and coordinating thread, make each ribbon into a folded leaf.

2. Cut three 11" lengths from ⅞"-wide ribbon. Refer to General Instructions for Tendril on page 18. Twist each ribbon into a tendril.

3. Cut three 18" lengths and one 24" length from ⅞"-wide ribbon. Refer to General Instructions for Rose on page 16. Make each ribbon into a rose, gathering along

light side of ribbon.

4. Cut one 18" length from ⅞"-wide ribbon. Make ribbon into a rose, gathering along dark side of ribbon.

5. Expose ends of wires on remaining 1½"-wide ribbon. Pull wires to gather ribbon into a 25" length. Set aside.

6. Using the outer edge of precut oval photo mat as a guide, trace two ovals onto heavy cardboard. Using a craft knife, cut out ovals.

7. Spray front of oval mat with spray adhesive. Cover mat with brown silk fabric. Cut excess fabric from inside and outside oval, leaving ¾" to turn under. Clip curves and fold fabric to back of mat. Secure fabric to back of mat using craft glue. Repeat process, covering front of cardboard ovals with taupe brocade fabric.

8. Lay gathered 25" length of ribbon around front of oval mat, aligning the darker edge of ribbon with outer edge of mat. Fit ribbon to mat by gathering inside ribbon edge more tightly and loosening outside edge. Evenly distribute gathers around mat. Using a hot-glue gun and glue sticks, secure ribbon to mat. Refer to Oval Frame Placement on page 86.

9. Glue brown decorative trim over inside edge of gathered ribbon. Glue brown gimp and taupe cording around outside edge.

10. Arrange and glue tendrils onto front of mat. Fold cut ends of folded leaves under and glue in place on tendrils.

There is nothing two people cannot do... if one of them is God.

11. Arrange and glue roses and remaining leaves onto front of mat.

12. With wrong sides together, glue fabric-covered ovals together. Glue gimp around seam of ovals.

13. Glue poster board strips around outer bottom and side edges of top fabric-covered oval. Glue back side of mat to strips only, leaving an opening for a photo. Insert photo.

Oval Frame Placement

Friend Pillow

Materials
Fabric: lt. blue taffeta (¼ yd.); lt. green taffeta (⅓ yd.)
Sheer ribbon: ⅞"-wide green with gold edges (⅓ yd.)
Wire-edge ribbon: ⅜"-wide gold mesh (¾ yd.); ⅝"-wide gold mesh (½ yd.); ⅞"-wide purple/blue ombré (1½ yds.), purple/green ombré (¾ yd.), green/teal ombré (1 yd.); 1½"-wide sheer cream with gold edges (¾ yd.); 2¼"-wide

gold net (¼ yd.)
Buckram: 3" square
Leaves: silk (2); velvet (4)
Ribbon rose: mauve swirl
Tatted lace: scraps
Trim: ⅜"- wide gold/black fringe (½ yd.)
Stuffing

General Supplies & Tools
Glue: craft
Hot glue gun and glue sticks
Iron/ironing board
Needle: hand-sewing
Scissors: fabric
Sewing machine
Straight pins
Thread: coordinating

Instructions

1. Enlarge Pattern A on page 88. Using fabric scissors and Pattern A, cut two hearts from lt. green taffeta fabric.

2. Cut a 5½" x 45" strip of lt. blue taffeta fabric. Fold fabric in half lengthwise and press folded edge. Machine-baste two rows of gathering stitches ¼" and ½" from selvages.

3. Taper each end of the ruffle by gathering and curving ends down to fit into the dip of the heart as shown in Diagram A. Continue gathering and pinning ruffle to fit around edge of heart.

Diagram A

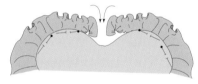

4. Sandwich ruffle between hearts and, with right sides together, machine-stitch hearts together, leaving an opening for turning and stuffing. Turn pillow right side out and loosely stuff. Using a hand-sewing needle and coordinating thread, stitch opening closed.

5. Diagonally lay gold net wire-edge ribbon across top of pillow front. Fold ribbon ends under. Tack ribbon to pillow front. Gently stretch ribbon into desired shape. Refer to Friend Pillow Placement on page 88.

6. Tack tatted lace in upper left corner and below gold net ribbon on pillow front.

7. Cut three 9" lengths from purple/blue ombré wire-edge ribbon. Refer to General Instructions for Pansy on page 15. Make two pansies with purple edges and one pansy with a blue edge.

8. Cut remaining purple/blue ombré wire-edge ribbon into six equal lengths. Refer to General Instructions for Single Petal on page 17. Make each ribbon into a petal, gathering two along the blue side and four along the purple side. Repeat process using sheer cream with gold edges wire-edge ribbon.

9. Cut gold/black fringe trim into three 2" lengths. Roll up each trim and secure with craft glue. Glue trim to center of each pansy.

10. Tack sheer cream with gold edges ribbon petals to purple/blue ombré ribbon petals. Tack blue petals to purple pansies and tack purple petals to blue pansy.

11. Refer to General Instructions for Buckram Rose on pages 10-11. Using buckram square and purple/green ombré ribbon, make a buckram rose.

12. Cut three 10" lengths from green/teal ombré ribbon. Refer to General Instructions for Gathered Leaf on page 13. Make each ribbon into a gathered leaf.

13. Cut ⅜"-wide gold mesh wire-edge ribbon into five equal lengths. Refer to General Instructions for Folded Leaf on page 12. Make each ribbon into a folded leaf.

14. Fold green with gold edges sheer ribbon into four loops. Tack ends together. Fold remaining gold/black fringe trim into two loops. Tack ends together.

15. Tie ⅜"-wide gold mesh wire-edge ribbon into a bow with 8" tails.

16. Using a black permanent marker, write

desired words or message on one silk leaf.

17. Using a hot glue gun and glue sticks, glue flowers.

leaves, looped ribbons, and bow onto pillow front as shown on Friendship Pillow Placement.

Friend Pillow Placement

Pattern A   Enlarge 200%

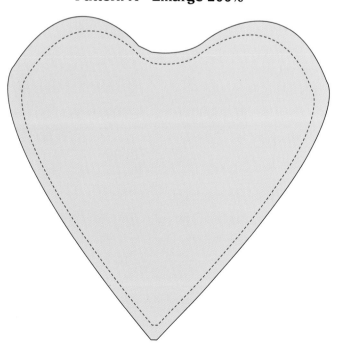

Flower Pillow

Note: Please refer to a book on basic embroidery stitches to complete this project.

Materials
Fabric: 10" x 12" ivory

Pillow: purchased, 16" square, moss/lt. moss green striped with ivory fringe

Wire-edge ribbon: ⅞"-wide green ombré (1¾ yds.); 1½"-wide purple ombré (3 yds.)

Ribbon roses: ivory swirl (3); ivory feather-edge (2); ivory large (5); ivory blooming (1)

Buttons: rhinestone, ⅜"-wide (8)

Lace collar: vintage

Lace glove

Pen: metallic gold paint

Trim: ⅜"-wide gold/black fringe (1¼ yds.)

General Supplies & Tools
Embroidery hoop

Embroidery floss: green

Fabric marker: air-soluble

Needle: embroidery; hand-sewing

Scissors: fabric

Thread: coordinating

Instructions
1. Refer to General Instructions for Transferring on page 9. Transfer verse using Flower Pillow Transfer

4. Cut ten 8" lengths from green ombré wire-edge ribbon. Refer to General Instructions for Gathered Leaf on page 13. Make each ribbon into a gathered leaf.

5. Turn edges of embroidered fabric under ½". Hem fabric. Diagonally place fabric onto pillow and stitch in place. Cover edge of fabric with gold/black fringe trim and stitch in place. Refer to Flower Pillow Placement.

6. Arrange flowers, leaves, lace collar, and glove on pillow top and tack in place.

7. Using a metallic gold paint pen, draw swirls onto pillow top.

Pattern on page 90 to center of ivory fabric. Place fabric in embroidery hoop.

2. Using an embroidery needle and green embroidery floss, embroider verse as desired onto fabric.

3. Using fabric scissors, cut eight 10½" lengths from purple ombré wire-edge ribbon. Fold dark edge of seven ribbons and light edge of one ribbon up ½". Divide each ribbon into five 2" sections with ¼" at each ribbon end. Refer to General

Instructions for Multiple-Petal Section on page 14. Make each folded ribbon into a five-petal section. Using a hand-sewing needle and co-ordinating thread, sew a button to center of each five-petal flower.

Flower Pillow Placement

Flower Pillow Transfer Pattern   Enlarge 200%

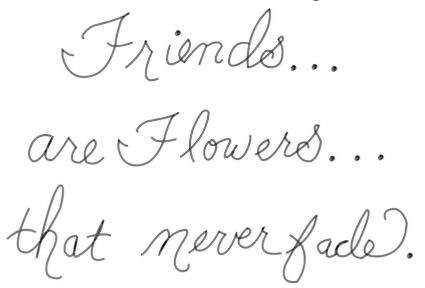

Friends...
are Flowers...
that never fade.

Rose Wreath

Materials

Grapevine wreath: 16"

Wire-edge ribbon: ⅜"-wide green ombré (1⅛ yds.); ⅞"-wide gold mesh (2 yds.), frosty rose (1⅛ yds.); 1½"-wide ivory taffeta (3 yds.), rose taffeta (4½ yds.), sheer cream with taupe edges (1¾ yds.), sheer cream with gold edges (2⅞ yds.); 1¾"-wide green sculptor (1⅜ yds.); 2¼"-wide gold net (1⅜ yds.)

Ribbon roses: mauve petal (2); ivory swirl (1); mauve swirl (3)

Buttons: ¾-1"-wide glass rhinestones (3)

Chenille stems (10)

Lace: 3"-wide ivory (¾ yd.)

General Supplies & Tools

Glue: craft

Hot glue gun and glue sticks

Needle: hand-sewing

Scissors: fabric

Skewer

Thread: coordinating

Instructions

1. Using fabric scissors, cut one 2½ yds. length and two 1 yd. lengths from rose taffeta wire-edge ribbon. Refer to General Instructions for Rose on page 16. Using a hand-sewing needle and co-ordinating thread, make each ribbon into a rose. Sew a rhinestone button in center of each rose.

2. Cut three 21½" lengths and one 35½" length from sheer cream with gold edges wire-edge ribbon. Divide each 21½" ribbon into three 7" sections and the 35½" ribbon into five 7" sections, with ¼" at each ribbon end. Refer to General Instructions for Multiple-Petal Section on page 14. Make each ribbon into a multiple-petal section. Pinch and shape each petal as desired. Sew a three-petal section around bottom of small roses and a three-petal and five-petal section around bottom of large rose.

3. Cut three 20½" lengths from sheer cream with taupe edges wire-edge ribbon. Divide each ribbon into five 4" sections with ¼" at each ribbon end. Refer to General Instructions for Multiple-Petal Section on page 14. Make each ribbon into a five-petal section. Pinch and shape each petal as desired. Using a glue gun and glue sticks, attach a mauve swirl ribbon rose in center of each five-petal section.

4. Cut three 1 yd. lengths from ivory taffeta wire-edge ribbon. Refer to General Instructions for Rose on page 16. Stitch each ribbon into a rose. Tightly pinch the top edges of the roses,

*I love to bring the roses in
and here count them dearest friends.*

Cut four 10" lengths from green ombré ribbon. Refer to General Instructions for Wrapped Bud on page 18. Wrap and stitch a ribbon around each bud.

8. Refer to General Instructions for Rosette on page 16. Make remaining frosty rose wire-edge ribbon into a rosette.

9. Cut three 9" lengths from lace. Sew a gather stitch around three sides of each lace piece. Pull gather and shape lace into a fan.

10. Arrange flowers, buds, leaves, tendrils, and lace fans on wreath and hot-glue in place as shown in Rose Wreath Placement.

drawing edges to center and pushing petals slightly upward.

5. Twist two chenille stems together to form five stems. Using craft glue, apply a small amount of glue at end of stem and begin wrapping stem with ⅞"-wide gold mesh wire-edge ribbon, securing ribbon to stem with glue. Repeat process on remaining stems. Tightly wrap stems around skewer to curl. Slide curled stems off skewer.

6. Cut seven 7" lengths

from green sculptor wire-edge ribbon and 2¼"-wide gold net wire-edge ribbon. Refer to General Instructions for Folded Leaf on page 12. Make each ribbon into a folded leaf.

7. Cut four 6" lengths from frosty rose wire-edge ribbon. Refer to General Instructions for Basic Bud on page 9. Make each ribbon into a bud.

Rose Wreath Placement

Blooming Fabric Frame

It is something to be able to paint a particular picture, or to carve a statue and so to make a few objects beautiful; But it is far more glorious to carve and paint the very atmosphere and medium through which we look. To affect the quality of the day... that is the highest of the arts.

—Henry David Thoreau

Materials
Fabric: taupe taffeta (½ yd.)
Photo mat: 11" x 14" precut rectangle
Poster board: 11" x 14" rectangle (2)
Sheer ribbon: ⅝"-wide pink with gold edge (¾ yd.)
Wire-edge ribbon: ⅝"-wide green with gold edge (¾ yd.); 1½"-wide brown ombré (1 yd.), green ombré (1¼ yds.), gold net (½ yd.), peach/green ombré (⅓ yd.), purple ombré (4½ yds.)
Brass charms, dragonfly: large (1), small (1)
Cording: ¼"-wide taupe (1 yd.)
Gimp: taupe (1½ yds.)
Lace: ⅞"-wide taupe (½ yd.); 3"-wide ivory (¼ yd.); 4"-wide ivory crocheted (¼ yd.)
Quilt batting: lightweight (½ yd.)
Rhinestones: ¼" (2); ⅜"

General Supplies & Tools
Glue: industrial strength; spray adhesive
Hot Glue gun and glue sticks
Needle: hand-sewing
Scissors: fabric
Thread: coordinating

Instructions
1. Spray front of photo mat with spray adhesive. Attach quilt batting to front of mat. Using fabric scissors, trim batting close to edges. Spray batting with spray adhesive. Cover batting with taffeta fabric. Trim fabric to within ¾" of inside and outside edges. Fold excess fabric to back of mat. Using a glue gun and glue sticks, secure excess fabric to back of mat.

2. Cover one side of poster board rectangles with remaining taffeta fabric. Trim fabric to within ¾" of outside edges. Fold excess fabric to back of poster board and hot-glue to secure. Hot-glue rectangle backs together and lay heavyweight object on top until dry.

3. Cut two 36" lengths from

purple ombré wire-edge ribbon. Refer to General Instructions for Rose on page 16. Using a hand-sewing needle and coordinating thread, make each ribbon into a rose.

4. Cut four 12" lengths from purple ombré wire-edge ribbon and one 12" length from peach/green ombré wire-edge ribbon. Refer to General Instructions for Multiple-Petal Section on page 14. Make each ribbon into a three-petal section, two with a dark purple edge, two with a light purple edge, and one with a green edge.

5. Cut two 3" lengths and two 7" lengths from remaining purple ombré wire-edge ribbon. Refer to General Instructions for Basic Bud on page 9. Make each 3" ribbon into a bud. Refer to General Instructions for Wrapped Bud on page 18. Wrap and stitch each 7" ribbon around the buds.

6. Cut gold net wire-edge ribbon into three equal lengths. Cut seven 6" lengths from green ombré wire-edge ribbon and nine 3" lengths from green with gold edge wire-edge ribbon. Refer to General Instructions for

Folded Leaf on page 12. Make each ribbon into a folded leaf.

7. Cut pink with gold edge sheer ribbon into three equal lengths. Divide each ribbon into five 1½" sections with ¼" at each ribbon end. Refer to General Instructions for Multiple-Petal Section. Make each ribbon into a five-petal section.

8. Cut brown ombré wire-edge ribbon into two equal lengths. Refer to General Instructions for Tendril on page 18. Twist each ribbon into a tendril.

9. Diagonally wrap 3"-wide ivory lace across top right corner of mat. Secure edges to underside of mat with hot glue. Diagonally wrap taupe lace across top right and bottom right corners of mat. Secure edges to underside of mat with hot glue. Gather one long edge of 4"-wide crocheted lace and shape over top left corner of mat. Secure gathered

edge to top of mat with hot glue. Refer to Blooming Fabric Frame Placement.

10. Glue cording around inside edge of photo mat.

11. Apply beads of hot glue around sides and bottom edges of rectangle back. Attach mat to rectangle back.

12. Glue gimp around seam of rectangle backs.

13. Arrange flowers, leaves and tendrils on front of mat and hot-glue in place.

14. Using industrial-strength glue, attach dragonflies to mat and rhinestones to center of each pink with gold edges five-petal section.

Blooming Fabric Frame Placement

Gilded Rose Frame

*Love is like
a beautiful flower
which I may not touch, but
whose fragrance makes the
garden a place of delight
just the same.*

—Helen Keller

glue sticks, hot-glue ribbon rose to center of folded flower.

3. Cut gold mesh wire-edge ribbon into seven equal lengths. Refer to General Instructions for Folded Leaf on page 12. Make each ribbon into a folded leaf.

4. Hot-glue folded flower to top center of frame. Hot-glue three folded leaves on each side of folded flower as shown in Gilded Rose Frame Placement.

5. Insert desired photo or inspirational message into frame.

Materials
Frame: purchased, 7" x 9" ecru fabric-covered
Sheer ribbon: ⅜"-wide lt. pink with gold edging (2 yds.)
Wire-edge ribbon: 1¼"-wide gold mesh (1¼ yds.)
Ribbon rose: cream swirl

General Supplies & Tools
Hot glue gun and glue sticks
Needle: hand-sewing
Scissors: fabric

Thread: coordinating

Instructions
1. Refer to General Instructions for Folded Flower on page 12. Using a hand-sewing needle and coordinating thread, stitch lt. pink with gold edging sheer ribbon into a folded flower.

2. Using a hot glue gun and

Gilded Rose Frame Placement

Vanessa-Ann

The Vanessa-Ann Collection has been, for more than 15 years, in the forefront of the needlework and craft industry. Working from offices in Ogden, Utah, the Vanessa-Ann staff is busy designing, packaging, and producing more than 20 hard-bound how-to publications per year.

Although best known for cross-stitch books, The Vanessa-Ann Collection, under the name "Chapelle Limited," has crossed over into almost every "craft" imaginable, from juggling to wood-working, rubber stamping to quilting, knot tying to music boxes.

A staff of 20 employees, as well as many free-lance designers, crafters, and stitchers, spend their days planning, painting, sewing, building, researching, editing, and photographing projects for upcoming books.

Instructions

1. Make one color copy of Pansy Art on page 122 at a copy center.

2. Using small, sharp craft scissors, cut pansies and greenery from color copied art. Place and arrange art in oval shape on back of one piece of glass, overlapping as necessary.

3. Following manufacturer's instructions, attach art to back of glass with reverse decoupage glue.

4. Using a router, make a ¼" groove down center of plywood base and dowel.

5. Using acrylic gesso and following manufacturer's instructions, seal all wood pieces. Refer to General Instructions for Painting Techniques on page 18. Paint wood pieces as follows: base paint all wood pieces ivory.

6. Following manufacturer's instructions, apply brown antiquing medium to all painted wood pieces.

7. Using matte spray sealer,

Note: Please refer to a book on basic embroidery stitches to complete this project.

Materials

Finials: 6½" curtain (2)
Plywood: ½" x 3" x 7"
Dowel: ½"-diameter (5¼")
Embroidery ribbon: 4mm yellow (⅜ yd.)
Wire-edge ribbon: ⅜"-wide green ombré, pink ombré, dk. purple ombré , lt. purple ombré (⅜ yd. each)
Acrylic gesso
Acrylic paint: ivory
Antiquing medium: brown
Glass: 5" x 7" (2)
Reverse decoupage glue
Spray sealer: matte finish

General Supplies & Tools

Hot glue gun and glue sticks
Needles: chenille; hand-sewing
Paintbrushes
Router
Scissors: craft, small sharp; fabric
Thread: coordinating

spray and seal all painted wood pieces.

8. Refer to Pansy Finial Frame Placement. Using a hot glue gun and glue sticks, attach finials to base.

9. Using fabric scissors, cut four 2¾" lengths from green ombré wire-edge ribbon. Refer to General Instructions for Fold-Over Leaf on page 12. Using a hand-sewing needle and coordinating thread, stitch each ribbon into a fold-over leaf.

10. Refer to General Instructions for Pansy on page 15. Stitch pink, dk. purple, and lt. purple ombré wire-edge ribbons into pansies.

11. Cut three 4½" lengths from yellow embroidery ribbon. Using a chenille needle, stitch a French Knot through center of each pansy.

12. Hot-glue pansies and leaves to front of glass that has been decoupaged.

13. Sandwich photo between glass pieces. Place dowel on top of glass pieces. Place glass in groove in base.

Pansy Finial Frame Placement

Pansy Board

Note: Please refer to a book on basic embroidery stitches to complete this project.

Materials
Drop ceiling tile
Embroidery ribbon: 4mm yellow (1¼ yds.)
Wire-edge ribbon: ⅝"-wide green ombré (⅝ yd.), orange ombré (⅞ yd.), dk. purple ombré (⅝ yd.), lt. purple ombré (⅜ yd.), yellow ombré (⅜ yd.); ⅞"-wide brown ombré (½ yd.), pink/purple ombré (½ yd.), yellow ombré (½ yd.); 1½"-wide green/pink ombré (1¼ yds.)
Acrylic paints: brown, green, ivory, yellow
Hot glue gun and glue sticks
Spray sealer: matte finish
Photo transfer medium

General Supplies & Tools
Craft knife
Needle: chenille; hand-sewing
Paintbrushes

6. Using a sponge and paper towel, blot ivory acrylic paint around edges of tile, and blend with art. Repeat process using yellow, then green, acrylic paint to create a mottled appearance. Allow to dry and then spray with matte acrylic.

7. Using fabric scissors, cut eight 2¾" lengths from green ombré wire-edge ribbon. Refer to General Instructions for Fold-Over Leaf on page 12. Using a hand-sewing needle and coordinating thread, stitch each ribbon into a fold-over leaf.

8. Cut ⅝"-wide and ⅞"-wide ombré wire-edge ribbons into the following lengths: brown — one 14" length; dk. purple — two 10" lengths; lt. purple — one 10" length; pink/purple — one 14" length; orange —three 10" lengths; yellow — ⅝"-wide, one 10" length, ⅞"-wide one 14" length. Refer to General Instructions for Pansy on page 15. Stitch each ribbon into a pansy.

Paper towels
Sponge
Sandpaper: medium grit
Scissors: craft, small sharp; fabric
Thread: coordinating

Instructions

1. Make a color copy of Pansy Art on page 122 at a copy center.

2. Using small, sharp craft scissors, cut desired number and shape of pansies and greenery from color copied art.

3. Using a craft knife, cut ceiling tile to desired size. Using medium grit sandpaper, round all edges of ceiling tile.

4. Following manufacturer's instructions, transfer pansies and greenery to ceiling tile using photo transfer medium.

5. Refer to General Instructions for Painting Techniques on page 18. Wash entire art and rounded edges of ceiling tile with brown acrylic paint.

9. Cut nine 4½" lengths from yellow embroidery ribbon. Using a chenille needle, stitch a French Knot through center of each pansy,

except for small yellow pansy.

10. Using a hot glue gun and glue sticks, attach leaves and pansies to tile as shown in Pansy Board Placement or as desired.

11. Tie a 7"-wide bow at center of green/pink ombré wire-edge ribbon. Hot-glue ribbon tails to back of tile for hanger.

Pansy Board Placement

Mini Hearts

Mini Heart—Sun

Note: Please refer to a book on basic embroidery stitches to complete this project.

Materials

Fabric: 9" x 11" white cotton

Embroidery ribbon: 4mm blue (1½ yds.), lt. green (1½ yds.), med. green (2½ yds.), mauve (1½ yds.), orange (2 yds.), yellow (1½ yds.); 7mm dk. red (1½ yds.)

Wire-edge ribbon: 3/8"-wide blue (½ yd.), mauve (1 yd.), pink (⅝ yd.)

Beads: 3mm pearls (15); 4 x 3mm brown (8); 8mm iridescent (4)

Embroidery floss: brown, green

General Supplies & Tools

Embroidery hoop
Needles: beading; chenille;
   embroidery; hand-sewing
Scissors: fabric
Thread: beading; coordinating

Instructions

1. Refer to General
Instructions for Transferring
Art to Fabric on page 9.
Transfer Mini Heart Art on
page 121 to cotton fabric.

2. Place fabric tightly in
embroidery hoop.

3. Using chenille,
embroidery, and beading
needles, embroider fabric
following Sun Stitch Guide
at right.

4. Cut four 8" lengths from
mauve wire-edge ribbon.
Refer to General Instructions
for Spiral Rosetta on page
17. Using a hand-sewing
needle and coordinating
thread, stitch each ribbon
into a spiral rosetta.

5. Cut four 4½" lengths from
blue wire-edge ribbon. Refer
to General Instructions for
Gathered Ruffle Flower on
page 13. Stitch each ribbon
into a gathered ruffle flower.
Using a beading needle and
beading thread, sew pearl

Mini Hearts—Sun Stitch Guide

	Description	Ribbon/Floss	Stitch
1.	Heart	blue	Whipped Running Stitch
2.	Circle	med. green	Whipped Running Stitch
3.	Square Border	mauve	Running Stitch
4.	Stem	green floss (6 strands)	Stem Stitch
5.	Leaf	green floss (3 strands)	Lazy Daisy Stitch
6.	Leaf	lt. green	Lazy Daisy Stitch
7.	Petal	blue	Ribbon Stitch
8.	Rose	yellow	Spider Web Rose
9.	Rose Bud	mauve	French Knot
10.	Rose	mauve	Spider Web Rose Stitch
11.	Butterfly Wing	dk. red	Lazy Daisy Stitch
12.	Antenna	brown floss (4 strands)	Straight Stitch
13.	Sun	orange	Ribbon Stitch
14.	Branch	green floss (3 strands)	Feather Stitch
15.	Leaf	med. green	Lazy Daisy Stitch
16.	Flower Center	iridescent beads	Beading Stitch
17.	Butterfly Body	brown beads	Beading Stitch
18.	Bead	pearl beads	Beading Stitch

Mini Hearts—Sun Stitch Guide

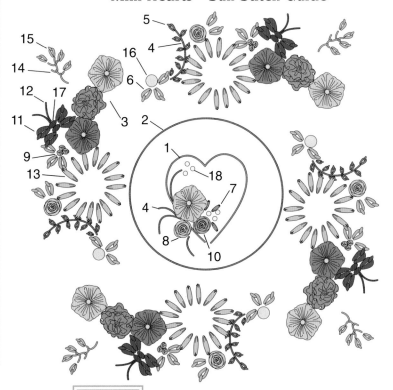

beads in center of flowers using a beading stitch. Repeat process using pink wire-edge ribbon.

6. Refer to Sun Placement on page 102. Using an embroidery needle and coordinating thread, tack rosettas and gathered ruffle flowers to design. Slightly overlap rosettas, flowers, and surrounding needlework.

7. Remove fabric from embroidery hoop.

8. Frame as desired.

Mini Heart—Rabbit

Materials
Fabric: 9" x 11" white cotton
Embroidery ribbon: 4mm
   lt. green (1 yd.),
   med. green (1 yd.), mauve
   (½ yd.), orange (1½ yds.)
   yellow (½ yd.),
Embroidery floss: blue

General Supplies & Tools
Embroidery hoop
Needles: chenille;
   embroidery
Scissors: fabric

Instructions
1. Refer to General Instructions for Transferring Art to Fabric on page 9. Transfer Mini Heart Art on page 121 to cotton fabric.

2. Place fabric tightly in embroidery hoop.

3. Using chenille and embroidery needles, embroider fabric following

Rabbit Stitch Guide below.

4. Remove fabric from embroidery hoop.

5. Frame as desired.

Mini Hearts—Rabbit Stitch Guide

	Description	Ribbon/Floss	Stitch
1.	Heart	blue floss (6 strands)	Outline Stitch
2.	Circle	med. green	Whipped Running Stitch
3.	Leaves	lt. green	Leaf Stitch
4.	Leaves	lt. green	Straight Stitch
5.	Rose	yellow	Spider Web Rose
6.	Rose Bud	yellow	French Knot
7.	Rose	mauve	Spider Web Rose
8.	Square Border	orange	Running Stitch

Mini Hearts—Rabbit Stitch Guide

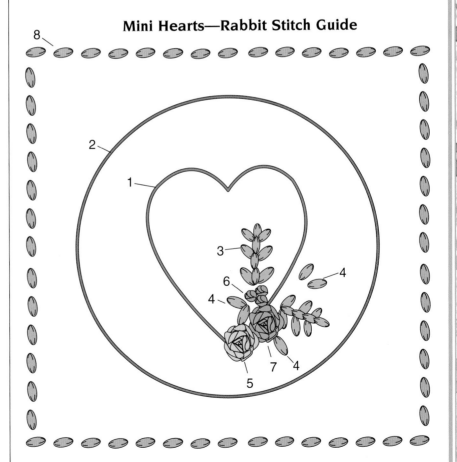

Mini Heart—Sun Placement

Mini Heart—Rabbit Placement

Floral Purse

Note: Please refer to a book on basic embroidery stitches to complete this project.

Materials

Embroidery ribbon: 4mm blue (½ yd.), dk. green (1⅛ yds.), lt. green (1 yd.), pale yellow (1 yd.); 7mm lt. green (2⅔ yds.), med. green (½ yd.), dk. red (1 yd.), gold (½ yd.)

Wire-edge ribbon: 1/2"-wide blue (⅝ yd.), red (⅓ yd.); 1½"-wide mauve (½ yd.)

Embroidery floss: green, gold

Beads: glass, 5mm pink faceted (6); 6mm clear round (28), purple round (7); 8mm purple round (6); 9mm pink faceted (1); 12mm purple round (1); ³⁄₁₆" purple bugle (4); ½" purple oblong (4), pink teardrop (6); 1" purple teardrop (1); seed, metallic pink (approx. 300), purple (17)

Cording: ⅛"-wide mauve (1½ yds.), lt. pink (1½ yds.)

Fabric: white linen (¼ yd.); muslin (¼ yd.)

Stamens: mauve (3)

General Supplies & Tools

Embroidery hoop
Needles: beading; chenille; embroidery; hand-sewing
Pencil
Scissors: fabric
Sewing machine
Thread: beading; coordinating

Instructions

1. Refer to General Instructions for Transferring on page 9. Transfer Pink Floral Art on page 125 to muslin fabric three times for purse front, purse back, and flap.

2. Enlarge Floral Purse Pattern on page 104. Using a pencil, trace purse front, purse back, and flap on white linen fabric. Cut out lining pieces.

3. Trace flap on one block of transferred art.

4. Place purse front portion of printed muslin fabric tightly in embroidery hoop.

5. Using chenille and embroidery needles, embroider purse front following Floral Purse Front Stitch Guide on page 105.

6. Place flap portion of printed muslin fabric tightly in embroidery hoop.

7. Embroider flap following Floral Purse Flap Stitch Guide on page 106.

8. Remove muslin fabric from embroidery hoop.

9. Using fabric scissors, cut out embroidered purse front and flap, and purse back.

10. Cut two 8" lengths and one 6" length from blue wire-edge ribbon. Refer to General Instructions for Boat Leaf on page 10. Using a

Diagram C

12. With right sides together and ½" seam, sew bottom of purse front and purse back together. Press seam open.

13. Using a pencil and beginning and ending at ½" seams, evenly mark intervals for bead spacing on seam as in Diagram D.

Diagram D

Bead Spacing

hand-sewing needle and coordinating thread, fold and stitch each ribbon into a boat leaf. Tack boat leaves to purse front referring to Floral Purse Placement on page 105.

11. Cut three 2" lengths and two 3" lengths from red wire-edge ribbon. Sew a gather stitch on 2" ribbons as shown in Diagram A. Pull gather to form petals and secure threads. Sew a gather stitch on 3" ribbons as shown in Diagram B. Pull gather to form petals and secure threads. Tack petals

to flap as shown in Diagram C and Floral Purse Placement on page 105.

Diagram A

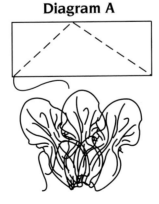

Diagram B

14. Refer to General Instructions for Bead Stringing on page 10. Using a beading needle and beading thread, string beads as shown in Diagram E on page 104. Sew strung beads through bottom seam and knot thread at marked intervals to attach to purse as shown in Floral Purse Placement on page 105.

Diagram E

15. With rights sides together and ½" seam, sew

sides of purse front and purse back together. Clip corners and turn right side out. Fold top inward ½" and press.

16. With right sides together and ½" seam, sew sides and point of flap lining and flap together. Clip corners and turn right side out. Carefully press edges. With ½" seam, stitch top of flap closed.

17. With right sides together and ½" seam, sew sides and bottom of lining front and lining back together. Clip corners and

turn right side out. Fold top inward ½" and press. Place lining inside purse and even up top edges of lining and purse.

18. Hold cording lengths together as one. Pin cording ends at side seams between lining and purse.

19. Place flap between lining and back of purse, making certain design on flap matches up with design on front of purse. With a ⅛" seam, sew around top of purse.

20. Cut three 5½" lengths from mauve wire-edge ribbon. Fold ribbons as shown in Diagram F. Whipstitch stamens to ribbons.

Floral Purse Pattern   Enlarge 200%

Bead Spacing

Cut Line

Stitch Line

Diagram F

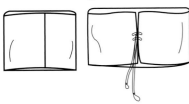

21. Sew a gather stitch on ribbons as shown in Diagram G. Pull gathers and secure threads to form fuchsias.

Diagram G

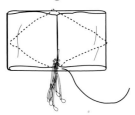

22. Tack fuchsias to flap as shown in Floral Purse Placement.

Floral Purse Placement

Floral Purse Front Stitch Guide

	Description	Ribbon/Floss	Stitch
1.	Flower Stem	gold floss (6 strands)	Stem Stitch
2.	Flower Stem	green floss (6 strands)	Stem Stitch
3.	Leaf Stem	4mm lt. green	Whipped Running Stitch
4.	Leaf	7mm lt. green	Lazy Daisy Stitch
5.	Leaf	pale yellow	Ribbon Stitch

Floral Purse Front Stitch Guide

Floral Purse Flap Stitch Guide

Description	Ribbon/Floss	Stitch
1. Leaf Stem	4mm lt. green	Whipped Running Stitch
2. Leaf	7mm lt. green	Lazy Daisy Stitch
3. Leaf Stem	dk. green	Whipped Running Stitch
4. Flower Stem	green floss (6 strands)	Stem Stitch
5. Flower Stem	gold floss (6 strands)	Stem Stitch
6. Leaf	dk. green	Lazy Daisy Stitch
7. Leaf	dk. green	Ribbon Stitch
8. Leaf	dk. green	Straight Stitch
9. Rosebud	dk. red	Lazy Daisy Stitch
10. Rosebud	dk. red	Ribbon Stitch
11. Leaf	med. green	Ribbon Stitch
12. Flower	blue	Lazy Daisy Stitch
13. Flower	blue	Straight Stitch
14. Garland	gold	Cascade Stitch
15. Arch	purple seed beads	Beading Stitch

Floral Purse Flap Stitch Guide

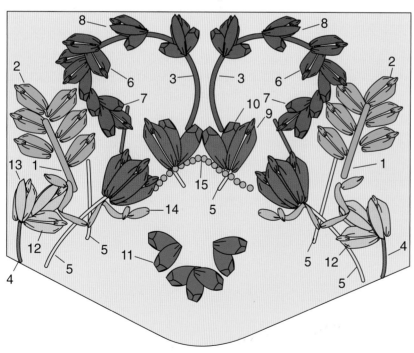

Note: Please refer to a book on basic embroidery stitches to complete this project.

Materials
Fabric: 11" x 17" white woven cotton; 15" x 23" canvas
Embroidery ribbon, 4mm: lt. blue, pale blue, green, dk. green, dusty green, mauve, orange, pink, purple, dusty purple, dk. rose
Embroidery floss: dk. green, lt. yellow
Beads: lt. yellow seed
Acrylic paint: ivory, mauve
Acrylic matte medium
Crackle medium
Gesso
Stretcher frame: 10" x 18"
Watercolor paint: Alazarian Crimson, Brown Madder

General Supplies & Tools
Needles: beading; chenille; embroidery
Paintbrushes
Pencil
Scissors: fabric
Staple gun and staples

Instructions
1. Refer to General Instructions for Transferring on page 9. Transfer Heart Art on pages 122-123 to white cotton fabric. Using fabric scissors and leaving a ½" allowance, cut out hearts.

8. Using ivory acrylic paint, paint on canvas around hearts. Let paint dry. Following manufacturer's instructions, apply crackle medium on canvas around hearts. Let crackle medium dry.

9. Cover work surface before painting canvas. Using a spare piece of canvas for practice, paint canvas with gesso, ivory acrylic paint and crackle medium. Allow canvas to dry after each application.

10. Mix equal amounts of Alazarian Crimson and Brown Madder watercolor paints. Using a large watercolor paintbrush, wet practice canvas. Apply watercolor mixture to canvas. Color should bleed slightly and may come off sides of canvas.

11. When desired look is obtained, wet project canvas around hearts. Apply watercolor mixture to canvas. Allow watercolors to bleed slightly onto edges of hearts as shown in photograph above. Let project dry completely.

12. Using mauve acrylic paint, paint sayings on

2. Stretch and tightly pull canvas over stretcher frame. Using a staple gun, secure canvas to stretcher frame.

3. Following manufacturer's instructions, apply gesso to top of canvas.

4. Place hearts on canvas following Canvas Hearts Placement on page 109. Using a pencil, lightly trace around hearts.

5. Using a paintbrush, paint a thin layer of acrylic matte

medium on inside area of each traced heart.

6. Set center of fabric hearts in center of traced hearts on canvas. Working outward, gently smooth hearts on canvas, using a paintbrush to gently press out air pockets. Wipe away any matte medium bleeding beyond hearts. Allow to dry.

7. Using beading, chenille, and embroidery needles, embroider hearts following Canvas Hearts Stitch Guide on page 108.

Canvas Hearts Stitch Guide

Description	Ribbon/Floss	Stitch
1. Heart Outline	lt. blue	Running Stitch
2. Heart Vine	orange	Fly Stitch
3. Rose	purple	Stem Stitch Rose
4. Rose Bud	purple	French Knot
5. Leaf	green	Ribbon Stitch
6. Leaf Branch	green	Leaf Stitch
7. Rose	dk. rose	Stem Stitch Rose
8. Rose	pink	Stem Stitch Rose
9. Leaf	dk. green	Ribbon Stitch
10. Stem	dk. green floss (3 strands)	Stem Stitch
11. Rose	mauve	Stem Stitch Rose
12. Forget-Me-Not Bud	pale blue	Loop Stitch
13. Forget-Me-Not Center	lt. yellow seed bead	Beading Stitch
14. Forget-Me-Not	lt. blue	Loop Petal Stitch
15. Forget-Me-Not Center	lt. yellow floss (3 strands)	French Knot
16. Rose	dusty purple	Stem Stitch Rose
17. Rose Bud	dusty purple	French Knot
18. Leaf Branch	dk. green	Leaf Stitch
19. Rose Bud	pink	French Knot
20. Rose Bud	dusty green	French Knot

Canvas Hearts Stitch Guide

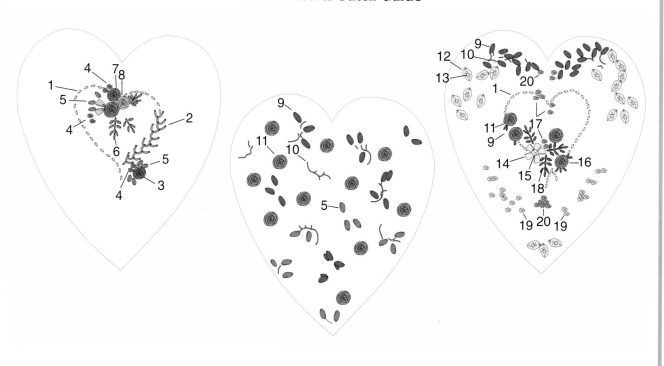

pages 125-126 on canvas as in Canvas Hearts Placement.

13. Cut one pink and two pale blue lengths of embroidery ribbon. Tie each in a bow and glue each bow on each heart cascading ribbon tails around each heart.

14. Hang or frame as desired.

Canvas Hearts Placement

Love is...time measured by the heart.

I have called a little flower my messenger to the let it whisper in thine ear all I would say to thee.

But the beating of my own heart was all the sound I heard.

Stocking

Note: Please refer to a book on basic embroidery stitches to complete this project.

Materials

Fabric: muslin (⅓ yd.)
Embroidery ribbon: 4mm brown (2 yds.), dk. brown (2 yds.), green (1½ yds.), dk. green (1½ yds.), red (1½ yds.); 7mm dk. red (2 yds.)
Wire-edge ribbon: ⅜"-wide red (¾ yd.); ⅝"-wide ivory (1 yd.); 2½"-wide ivory with gold edges (½ yd.)
Beads: 3mm round gold (64); ³⁄₁₆" clear bugle (38), gold bugle (78); ⅜" clear oval faceted (14); ⅝" frosted gold heart (5): gold seed (approximately 150)
Embroidery floss: brown
Thread: braided metallic gold

General Supplies & Tools

Embroidery hoop
Needles: beading; chenille; embroidery; hand-sewing
Pencil
Sewing machine
Scissors: fabric
Thread: beading; coordinating

Instructions

1. Refer to General Instructions for Transferring Art to Fabric on page 9. Transfer Poinsettia Art on page 125 to muslin fabric.

2. Enlarge Stocking & Cuff Transfer Pattern on page 111. Using a pencil, trace stocking on printed muslin for stocking front and on plain muslin fabric for stocking back.

3. Place stocking front tightly in embroidery hoop.

4. Using chenille, embroidery, and beading needles, embroider poinsettias following Stocking Stitch Guide on page 112.

5. Remove stocking front from embroidery hoop. Using fabric scissors, cut out stocking front and back.

6. With ¼" seam and right sides together, sew stocking front and stocking back together. Clip curves and turn right side out.

7. Cut three 5" lengths from ivory with gold edges wire-edge ribbon. Turn one end of each ribbon up ¼". Using a hand-sewing needle and coordinating thread, fold and tack ribbon ends as shown in Diagram A on page 110.

109

Diagram A

8. Place wrong sides of two tacked ribbons together. Using metallic gold thread, make a running stitch seam as shown in Diagram B. Repeat process with remaining tacked ribbon.

Diagram B

9. Cut a 12" x 4" strip of muslin for stocking cuff. Turn one long edge up ¼". Fold turned edge up ¼" and hem.

10. Mark center and ¼" seams on stocking cuff as shown in Diagram C.

Diagram C

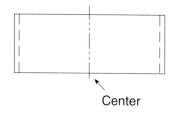

Center

11. Baste tacked ribbons on left side of stocking cuff. Sew a running stitch with gold metallic thread along three ribbon seams as shown in Diagram D.

Diagram D

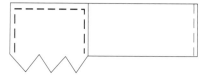

12. Using enlarged Stocking & Cuff Transfer Pattern on opposite page, center and transfer cuff pattern to ivory ribbon, leaving a ½" hem allowance at top.

13. Place stocking cuff tightly in embroidery hoop.

14. Embroider stocking cuff following Cuff Stitch Guide on page 112.

15. Remove stocking cuff from embroidery hoop.

16. With ¼" seam, sew right side of stocking cuff to wrong side of stocking. Turn stocking cuff right side out.

17. Remove basting thread. Sew a running stitch with gold metallic thread across top front of stocking cuff.

18. Refer to General Instructions for Bead Stringing on page 10. Using a beading needle and beading thread, string beads as shown in Diagram E, stringing clear and gold bugle beads as desired.

Diagram E

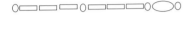

19. Sew bead strings with frosted gold heart beads at two center top and three bottom points of stocking cuff. Sew bead strings with clear oval beads at ½" intervals as shown in Diagram F.

Diagram F

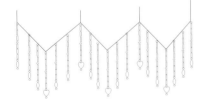

20. Sew 3mm round gold beads along pointed edge of stocking cuff as shown in Diagram G.

Diagram G

21. Cut six 4" lengths from red wire-edge ribbon. Refer to General Instructions for Boat Leaf on page 10. Fold and stitch each ribbon into a boat leaf. Sew leaves together to form a poinsettia. Sew seed beads in center of poinsettia.

22. Refer to General Instructions for Multi-Loop Bow on page 14. Tie ⅜"-wide ivory wire-edge ribbon into a multi-loop bow. Tack bow to top left corner of stocking cuff. Tack poinsettia to center of bow.

Stocking & Cuff Transfer Pattern   Enlarge 190%

Stocking Stitch Guide

	Description	Ribbon/Floss	Stitch
1.	Lg. Poinsettia Leaf	dk. red	Lazy Daisy Stitch
2.	Lg. Poinsettia Leaf	dk. red	Straight Stitch
3.	Lg. Poinsettia Leaf	dk. red	Ribbon Stitch
4.	Small Poinsettia Leaf	red	Lazy Daisy Stitch
5.	Small Poinsettia Leaf	red	Straight Stitch
6.	Small Poinsettia Leaf	red	Ribbon Stitch
7.	Poinsettia Center	gold seed beads	Beading Stitch

Stocking Stitch Guide

Cuff Stitch Guide

Stocking Placement

Cuff Stitch Guide

	Description	Ribbon/Floss	Stitch
1.	Branch	brown floss (6 strands)	Stem Stitch
2.	Pine Needle	green	Straight Stitch
3.	Pine Needle	dk. green	Straight Stitch
4.	Pine Cone	brown and dk. brown	Cretan Stitch

Angel Wreath

on page 9. Transfer Angel Art on page 32 to cotton fabric.

2. Place fabric tightly in embroidery hoop. Using embroidery, chenille, and beading needles, embroider fabric following Angel Wreath Stitch Guide on page 114.

3. Tie a 3"-wide bow from red wire-edge ribbon. Cut ribbon ends on a diagonal. Refer to General Instructions for Cascading on page 11. Tack bow in place following Angel Wreath Placement on page 114. Cascade ribbon.

4. Cut six 8½" lengths from pale yellow wire-edge ribbon. Refer to General Instructions for Multiple-Petal Section on page 14. Using a hand-sewing needle and coordinating thread, stitch each ribbon into a multiple-petal section.

5. Cut four 5" lengths from white satin wire-edge ribbon. Refer to General Instructions for Gathered Ruffle Flower on page 13. Stitch each ribbon into a gathered ruffle flower.

Note: Please refer to a book on basic embroidery stitches to complete this project.

Materials

Fabric: 16" square white cotton

Embroidery ribbon: 4mm dk. green (6 yds.), red (2 yds.)

Wire-edge ribbon: ⅜"-wide red (1⅛ yds.); ⅜"-wide white satin (⅝ yd.); 1"-wide pale yellow (1½ yds.)

Beads: red, 5mm-8mm assorted wood, glass, and faceted (20-30)

General Supplies & Tools

Embroidery hoop

Needles: beading; chenille; embroidery; hand-sewing

Scissors: fabric

Thread: coordinating

Instructions

1. Refer to General Instructions for Transferring

6. Tack flowers to design following Angel Wreath Placement.

7. Remove fabric from embroidery hoop. Frame or mount as desired.

Angel Wreath Placement

Angel Wreath Stitch Guide

	Description	Ribbon	Stitch
1.	Pine Needles	dk. green	Twisted Ribbon Stitch
2.	Ribbon	red	Twisted Ribbon Stitch
3.	Berries	beads	Beading Stitch

Angel Wreath Stitch Guide

Cards

Note: Cards used on this project were hand-painted.

Materials

Card: blank, floral motif

Cardstock: 5½" x 3¼" floral motif (1)

Ribbon roses: small (14); large (2); swirl (3)

Wire-edge ribbon: 1"-wide gold mesh (½ yd.)

General Supplies & Tools

Hot glue gun and glue sticks

Paper punch

Scissors: craft

Instructions

1. Referring to Card Placement, randomly hot-glue 11 small, two large, and two swirl ribbon roses to floral motif on card.

2. Cut gold ribbon into two equal lengths. Hold ribbons together as one and tie into a bow. Spread bow loops apart and shape ribbon tails. Cut tails on a diagonal. Hot-glue bow where desired on card.

3. Referring to Tag Placement, randomly hot-glue one swirl and three small ribbon roses to floral motif on cardstock rectangle. Trim two corners. Punch hole.

Angel Finial

Materials

Finial, wooden curtain
Embroidery ribbon: 7 mm
    green (2 yds.)
Satin ribbon: ⅟₁₆"-wide
    burgundy (1 yd.)
Wire-edge ribbon: ⅜"-wide
    burgundy (1⅛ yds.); ⅝"-
    wide ivory (¼ yd.); ⅞"-wide
    pale yellow (⅜ yd.)
Acrylic paints: dk. green,
    lt. green, red
Ball: wooden, 6½"-diameter
Beads: wooden, ⅜", ¾"
Cording: ⅛"-wide dk. green
    (1¼ yds.)
Poster board (4½" x 7")
Spray sealer: matte finish

General Supplies & Tools

Gesso
Glue: craft
Hot glue gun and glue sticks
Needle: hand-sewing
Paintbrushes
Pencil
Scissors: craft; fabric
Thread: coordinating

Instructions

1. Make two color copies of
Angel Art on page 124 at a
copy center.

2. Following manufacturer's
instructions, apply gesso to
all wood pieces.

Card Placement

Tag Placement

6. Using fabric scissors, cut two 12" lengths and one 14" length from dk. green cording. Fold 14" length in half and tie a knot at cut ends. Cut ends off close to knot and hot-glue to top of finial.

7. Cut one 22" length and one 17" length from burgundy wire-edge ribbon. Tie 17" ribbon around top of finial. Tie 22" ribbon into a bow with 4" tails around top of finial. Wrap all ribbon tails around pencil to curl. Remove pencil and let ribbon tails fall down finial.

8. Refer to Oval Pattern on opposite page. Trace two oval patterns onto posterboard. Center and trace oval onto both angel color copies. Using craft scissors, cut along tracing lines on color copies and posterboard. Using craft glue, glue angel color copies onto each oval poster board. To prevent curling while drying, place under a flat, heavy object.

9. Using fabric scissors, cut two 36" lengths from green embroidery ribbon. Refer to General Instructions for Fluting on page 12. Flute and glue one length of ribbon around back outside edge of each oval.

10. Glue 12" lengths of dk. green cording around front outside edge of each oval.

11. Fold remaining dk. green cording in half to form a loop. Center and glue cut ends of loop to top back of one oval. Glue backs of ovals together and allow to dry under flat, heavy object.

12. Cut ivory wire-edge ribbon into two 4½" lengths. Refer to General Instructions for Gathered Ruffle Flower on page 13. Using a hand-sewing needle and coordinating thread, stitch each ribbon into a gathered ruffle flower.

13. Cut two 6½" lengths from pale yellow wire-edge ribbon. Refer to General Instructions for Multiple-Petal Section on page 14. Stitch each ribbon into a multiple-petal section.

14. Glue a yellow and a white flower to top front and back of oval.

15. Cut burgundy satin ribbon into two equal lengths. Attach centers of ribbons to each side of cord loop at top of oval and tie into bows with looping tails. Randomly secure tails to

3. Refer to General Instructions for Painting Techniques on page 18. Paint all wood pieces as follows: base —⅜" bead and ball red, ¾" bead and finial dk. green; dry brush — all dk. green painted surfaces lt. green.

4. Using matte spray sealer, spray and seal all painted wood pieces.

5. Using a hot glue gun and glue sticks, glue painted wood pieces together as shown in Angel Finial Placement on opposite page.

oval with a small amount of glue.

16. Place a small amount of hot glue into bead hole at bottom of finial. Thread cord loop into hole to attach oval to finial.

Angel Finial Placement

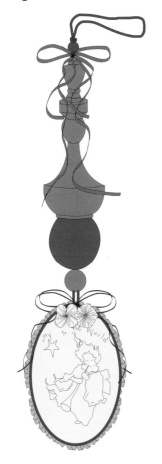

Oval Pattern   Enlarge 260%

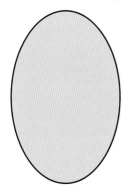

Materials
Clay pots: as desired
Wire-edge ribbon: ⅜"-wide white taffeta (4⅜ yds.); 1½"-wide – white taffeta (2 yds.); ⅞"-wide orange ombré taffeta (⅜ yds.), green ombré taffeta (3 yds.); ⅞" green ombré taffeta (4½ yds.)
Florist tape: pale green
Moss
Oasis: to fit inside clay pots
Stamens: red/white, pear (9), yellow (9)
Stem wire: 16-18 gauge

General Tools & Supplies
Glue: craft
Needles: hand-sewing
Scissors: fabric
Thread: coordinating
Wire cutters

Instructions
1. Refer to Steps 5-9 for Blossom Vase on page 68 to create branches.

2. Using fabric scissors, cut 1½"-wide wire-edge white ribbon into two 21" lengths. Refer to General Instructions for Stitched Flower on page 17, marking each length into six 3½" intervals.

3. Using wire cutters, cut two 9" pieces of stem wire. Attach red and white stamens to a stem wire.

4. Cut orange ombré wire-edge into two 4" pieces. Refer to General Instructions for Trumpet on page 18. Make each ribbon into a trumpet. Insert stamen in center of orange trumpet. Secure stamens in trumpet with a small amount of glue.

5. Cut ⅞"green ombré wire-edge ribbon into two 12" lengths. Refer to General Instructions for Boat Leaf on page 10. Make each ribbon into a boat leaf.

6. Refer to General Instructions for Narcissus on page 14. Make two narcissus.

7. Arrange apple blossoms branches and two narcissus in clay pots as shown on Flower Pot Placement. Cover oasis with moss.

Flower Pot Placement

Pansy Frame

Materials
Frame: 5" x 7" wood, crest-shaped

Wire-edge ribbon: ⅞"-wide olive green ombré taffeta (1 yd.); ⅞"-wide olive green ombré taffeta (6¾ yds.); 1½"-wide purple taffeta (⅜ yd.), yellow ombré taffeta (½ yd.)

Beads: black oval (2)

Quilt batting: 8"x 8" lightweight

General Supplies & Tools
Hot glue gun and glue sticks

Needles: hand-sewing

Pencil

Scissors: fabric

Thread: coordinating

Instructions
1. Using pencil, trace frame and opening onto quilt batting. Using fabric scissors, cut out frame shape from quilt batting.

2. Using hot glue gun and glue stick, attach quilt batting to front of frame.

3. Using ⅞"-wide olive green ombré wire-edge ribbon, wrap frame completely covering quilt batting.

Secure ribbon ends on back with hot glue.

4. Cut ⅞"-wide olive green ombré wire-edge ribbon into one 5" length and three 9" lengths. Refer to General Instructions for Pulled Petal or Leaf on page 15. Make each ribbon into a pulled leaf.

5. Cut purple wire-edge ribbon in half. Fold each ribbon in half. Refer to General Instructions for

Stitched Flower on page 17. Make each ribbon into a 2-petal stitched flower.

6. Cut yellow ombré wire-edge ribbon into two equal lengths. Mark each ribbon into thirds. Make each ribbon into a stitched flower. Tack first petal to third petal on each flower.

7. Sew a purple stitched flower to each yellow stitched flower to form a pansy.

8. Glue black oval bead to center of each pansy. Glue pansies and leaves onto left side of frame as shown on Pansy Frame Placement.

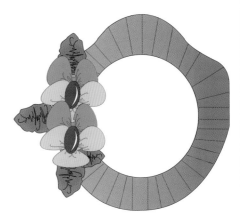

Pansy Frame Placement

Iris Mirror

Materials

Mirror: 18" oval wicker
Sheer ribbon: ⅝"-wide yellow (4½ yds.)
Wire-edge ribbon: ⅝"-wide olive green ombré taffeta (1⅜ yds.); 1½"-wide pink/purple ombré taffeta (1½ yds.), purple/blue taffeta (2⅞ yds.)
Florist tape: dk. green
Florist wire: 16-18 gauge, covered
Moss
Paddle wire: 24-26 gauge
Willow branches or twigs

General Supplies & Tools

Hot glue gun and glue sticks
Needles: hand-sewing
Scissors: fabric
Thread: coordinating

Instructions

1. Using fabric scissors, cut olive green ombré wire-edge ribbon into four equal lengths. Refer to General Instructions for Boat Leaf on page 10. Make each ribbon into a boat leaf.

2. Cut pink/purple ombré wire-edge ribbon into three 8" lengths. Make each ribbon into a petal, using boat leaf technique, and stitching along purple edge of ribbon.

3. Cut remaining pink/purple ombré wire-edge ribbon into three 9" lengths. Refer to General Instructions for Pulled Petal or Leaf on page 15. Pull wire on pink edge of ribbon. Make each ribbon into a pulled petal.

4. Cut purple/blue ombré wire-edge ribbon into six 8" lengths. Refer to General Instructions for Boat Leaf on page 10. Make each ribbon into a petal, using boat leaf technique and stitching along dark purple edge of ribbon.

5. Cut remaining purple/blue ombré wire-edge ribbon into six 9" lengths. Refer to General Instructions for Pulled Petal or Leaf on page

15. Make each ribbon into a pulled petal. Pull wire on light purple edge of ribbon.

6. Cut yellow sheer ribbon into nine 18" lengths. Sew a running stitch down center of each ribbon. Tightly gather each ribbon to 2-3" lengths. Using hot glue gun and glue stick, attach one gathered ribbon to center of each pulled petal as shown in Diagram A.

Diagram A

7. Using wire cutters, cut florist wire into three 9" lengths.

8. Assemble remaining petals into two clusters of three purple petals and one cluster of three pink petals. Glue tip of each petal cluster together. Turn petals outward and fold tips downward as shown in Diagram B. Insert stem wire into center of cluster. Secure base with a small piece of paddle wire.

Diagram B

9. Match colors of petal clusters with three pulled petals to form irises. Position each pulled petal between petals of each cluster as shown in Diagram C.

Diagram C

10. Secure all petals together with small piece of paddle wire. Wrap florist wire with dk. green florist tape, adding leaves to wires.

11. Fold pulled petals downward. Arrange and glue irises onto mirror. Glue moss and twigs to mirror. Refer to Iris Mirror for Placement.

Iris Mirror Placement

Mini Heart Art   Enlarge 150%

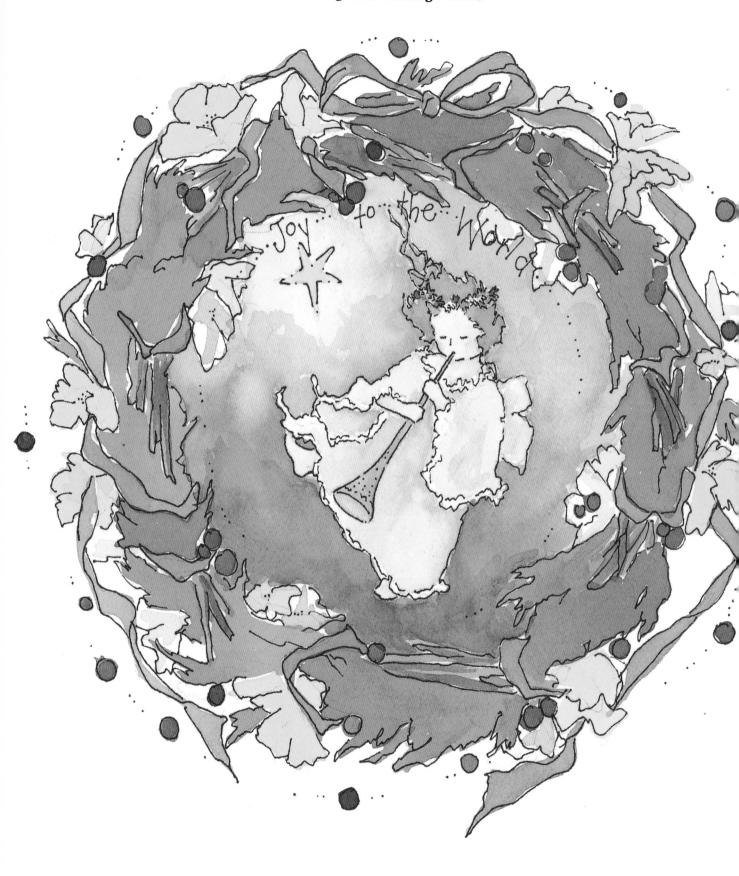

Heart Art   Enlarge 115%

I have called a little flower
my messenger to be
let it whisper in thine ear
all I would say to thee.

Pink Floral Art   Actual Size

But the beating of my own
heart was all the sound I
heard.

Love is...time measured
by the heart.

Metric Equivalency Chart

mm-millimetres cm-centimetres
inches to millimetres and centimetres

inches	mm	cm	inches	cm	inches	cm
⅛	3	0.3	9	22.9	30	76.2
¼	6	0.6	10	25.4	31	78.7
½	13	1.3	12	30.5	33	83.8
⅝	16	1.6	13	33.0	34	86.4
¾	19	1.9	14	35.6	35	88.9
⅞	22	2.2	15	38.1	36	91.4
1	25	2.5	16	40.6	37	94.0
1¼	32	3.2	17	43.2	38	96.5
1½	38	3.8	18	45.7	39	99.1
1¾	44	4.4	19	48.3	40	101.6
2	51	5.1	20	50.8	41	104.1
2½	64	6.4	21	53.3	42	106.7
3	76	7.6	22	55.9	43	109.2
3½	89	8.9	23	58.4	44	111.8
4	102	10.2	24	61.0	45	114.3
4½	114	11.4	25	63.5	46	116.8
5	127	12.7	26	66.0	47	119.4
6	152	15.2	27	68.6	48	121.9
7	178	17.8	28	71.1	49	124.5
8	203	20.3	29	73.7	50	127.0

yards to metres

yards	metres	yards	metres	yards	metres	yards	metres	yards	metres
⅛	0.11	2⅛	1.94	4⅛	3.77	6⅛	5.60	8⅛	7.43
¼	0.23	2¼	2.06	4¼	3.89	6¼	5.72	8¼	7.54
⅜	0.34	2⅜	2.17	4⅜	4.00	6⅜	5.83	8⅜	7.66
½	0.46	2½	2.29	4½	4.11	6½	5.94	8½	7.77
⅝	0.57	2⅝	2.40	4⅝	4.23	6⅝	6.06	8⅝	7.89
¾	0.69	2¾	2.51	4¾	4.34	6¾	6.17	8¾	8.00
⅞	0.80	2⅞	2.63	4⅞	4.46	6⅞	6.29	8⅞	8.12
1	0.91	3	2.74	5	4.57	7	6.40	9	8.23
1⅛	1.03	3⅛	2.86	5⅛	4.69	7⅛	6.52	9⅛	8.34
1¼	1.14	3¼	2.97	5¼	4.80	7¼	6.63	9¼	8.46
1⅜	1.26	3⅜	3.09	5⅜	4.91	7⅜	6.74	9⅜	8.57
1½	1.37	3½	3.20	5½	5.03	7½	6.86	9½	8.69
1⅝	1.49	3⅝	3.31	5⅝	5.14	7⅝	6.97	9⅝	8.80
1¾	1.60	3¾	3.43	5¾	5.26	7¾	7.09	9¾	8.92
1⅞	1.71	3⅞	3.54	5⅞	5.37	7⅞	7.20	9⅞	9.03
2	1.83	4	3.66	6	5.49	8	7.32	10	9.14

INDEX